Englischer Fussball

Raphael Honigstein was born in 1973 in Munich.
football correspondent for *Süddeutsche*
a columnist for the *Guardian*. He has
in London since 1993.

D0317522

Englischer Fussball

A German View of Our Beautiful Game

Raphael Honigstein

Translated from the German
by Jamie Bulloch

Yellow Jersey Press
LONDON

Published by Yellow Jersey Press 2009

4 6 8 10 9 7 5

Copyright © Raphael Honigstein 2009
Translation copyright © Jamie Bulloch 2009

Raphael Honigstein has asserted his right under the Copyright, Designs
and Patents Act 1988 to be identified as the author of this work

This book is sold subject to the condition that it shall not,
by way of trade or otherwise, be lent, resold, hired out,
or otherwise circulated without the publisher's prior
consent in any form of binding or cover other than that
in which it is published and without a similar condition,
including this condition, being imposed on the
subsequent purchaser

First published in Great Britain in 2009 by
Yellow Jersey Press
Random House, 20 Vauxhall Bridge Road,
London SW1V 2SA

www.rbooks.co.uk

Addresses for companies within The Random House Group Limited can be found at:
www.randomhouse.co.uk/offices.htm

The Random House Group Limited Reg. No. 954009

A CIP catalogue record for this book
is available from the British Library

ISBN 9780224080132

The Random House Group Limited makes every effort to ensure that the papers used in
its books are made from trees that have been legally sourced from well-managed and
credibly certified forests. Our paper procurement policy can be found at:
www.rbooks.co.uk/environment

Mixed Sources
Product group from well-managed
forests and other controlled sources
www.fsc.org Cert no. TT-COC-2139
© 1996 Forest Stewardship Council
FSC

Typeset by SX Composing DTP, Rayleigh, Essex
Printed and bound in Great Britain by
CPI Mackays, Chatham ME5 8TD

For Elinor and Robbie

LONDON BOROUGH OF HACKNEY	
913 000 00101168	
HJ	15-Oct-2010
796.334 HON	£11.99
DAC	

Contents

Introduction

It was a dull, throbbing pain which didn't match the wound. There was still a flap of skin, which you could easily push to one side, hanging limply over a hole the size of a fingertip. Deep in the red hollow something shone white – that had to be the shinbone. After I'd waited for four hours in the bright-blue casualty room, a man of about fifty arrived, half bald and with a twirly moustache. Some sort of medal was pinned above the breast pocket of his green work coat, it was impossible to tell what for. 'All right,' he said confidently, 'we won't have to stitch this; we'll stick it back together.' He took two small strips of plaster from a box and used them to press the flap of skin over the hole in my right leg. A pat on the shoulder and I was discharged.

Two weeks later the injury still hadn't healed. The flap of skin continued to hang flaccidly over the wound, and from beneath it yellow pus oozed forth every few days. I went to Norwich with an old school friend to watch Bayern Munich play. Fortunately we had to pay for the bed and breakfast in advance: the morning after Bayern were knocked out, half the bed sheet was soaked in blood. The wound had opened up again.

I can't remember whether it had happened in my second or third game for the University College London seconds. I can't really remember who the opponents were, either. It might have been King's College thirds, or the Imperial College second team. It was definitely a home game, at a ground in Hertfordshire where Arsenal trained at the time.

By English standards it had been an ordinary match. In other words, my opposite number hadn't quite rammed his iron studs half an inch deep into my skin on purpose (the shin pad had been knocked aside by the force of the impact). The mass of blood looked good on my blue socks, I thought. Unfortunately it hurt like hell, too. Was it a foul? I don't think so – there weren't any fouls in this game. The referee can't have blown his whistle more than three times throughout the whole match.

Just before the kick-off our captain, Duncan, had told me I was to play as an attacking midfielder. In practice that meant nothing more than chasing the ball from a particular area on the pitch. Showing for it – or, to be more precise, screaming your head off – was all-important. In Germany it was the opposite: you were told to keep quiet and play with your head up.

The boys were not only ten times harder than those at home, but fitter as well. As soon as you took possession of the ball, studs would fly at you from both sides. This was football, perhaps, but not as I knew it.

I only had a few more games before the winter vacation. At the Christmas party I disappointed my team-mates because it took me more than ten seconds to drink my pint in the 'boat race', a kind of drinking relay. 'You really are from Germany?' Duncan wondered, shaking his head disparagingly. He'd brought his girlfriend along to the party. It wasn't long before the boys started serenading her with a rendition of 'Get your tits out for the lads!'. They were joking but really meant it all the same. She didn't oblige. Duncan smiled gleefully.

After that I didn't play many more times for the university. I soon discovered that even during a Sunday knockabout in Regent's Park you'd be tackled to bits in this country. While on neighbouring pitches Kurds, Saudis and Brazilians would kick it about nonchalantly on small pitches, the English would run one another into the ground and steam into each bone-crunching challenge with a happy sense of abandon. For them, that was the essence of the game. Curiously, the foreigners would always have more arguments; time and again their matches stopped because of a disagreement or a minor tussle. The English would just go on, and on, and on.

Harder, better, faster, stronger, as the song (and the original title of the German version of this book) goes: the whole world loves English football for these very characteristics. But why is it that the English find 'the beautiful game' most attractive when it becomes a fight to the death? Where does this incredible sense of aggression on the pitch and in the stands come from? The aim of this book is to figure out why football in England is as it is – so different, so unique, so violent, and so damned attractive for players, supporters and worldwide television audiences.

When you delve deeper into the origins of the sport, you uncover a strong yet secretive narrative. English football tells a story about itself, about England and the rest of the world, albeit in an almost involuntary fashion. Some of it is a little troubling and altogether left unsaid. A few of these peculiar hang-ups and preoccupations were familiar to me, as they are shared by the sport in Germany. Many more weren't.

Football's genetic make-up shines through this strange story: ancient myths, Protestant values, sexual repression and the ideal of manhood in the Victorian age. Back then the game was introduced by ultra-strict headmasters as occupational therapy for frustrated boarding-school boys. Ever since the working class made the sport their own a century ago, two contrary but at the same time complementary phenotypes have been dominating the pitch. On the one side there is the noble knight who sets the example of conduct and fair play, and who defends the values of the upper class; on the other side the unassuming, courageous warrior is venerated. As an English footballer, you can be one or the other. Artists or technicians have traditionally had a hard time by contrast.

I spoke to football academics John Williams (Leicester) and John Sugden (Bournemouth) about the mimetic war games of fans and the influence of fashion and pop music; and to English journalists about the most efficient, terrifying press on the planet. I visited most Premier League grounds, and Elland Road. I experienced the Champions League final in Istanbul with Liverpool FC and thousands of Scousers; I shadowed the English national team at the European Championship in Portugal and the World Cup in Germany. German players toughened up by the Premier League, such as Thomas Hitzlsperger, Jens Lehmann, Didi Hamann and Robert Huth, told me about the incomparable hardness, the insane pace on the pitch, explained to me why diving is frowned upon. They did mention the war, too: England's complex relationship with Germany is never more visual than on the football pitch.

In Geneva, I once got on a bus full of drunken Englishmen who sang 'There are ten German bombers in the sky, and the RAF from England shot them down' until the windows became fogged up. Two young Swiss men were interrogated as to why they had not fought against the 'Krauts' during the war.

I flew to Thailand to watch the country's most important derby – Liverpool against Manchester United – and saw a packed sports hall where 7,000 Thais in two neatly separated blocks started screaming whenever a young hooligan by the name of Rooney took possession of the ball 6,000 miles away. 'Italy has the tactical league, Spain the technical one,' José Mourinho, then the Chelsea manager, told me. 'And in England passion dominates.' But for how much longer? The world described on the following pages is already disappearing.

Unparalleled income from television rights, ticket sales and merchandising, and club structures that facilitate foreign investment have made the Premier League the richest league in the world. As far as the top flight is concerned, football in Britain is more thoroughly globalised than anywhere else. It is not just the best players who now mostly come from abroad, but the managers, too; this is also fast becoming true of the club owners. People are worried that the very cornerstones of English football – hardness and pace – are being pushed aside by continental sophistication.

This impending loss of identity troubles the English. Since the decline of the Empire, if not earlier, they have been a nation of nostalgia junkies, and the stuff their dreams are made of has always been laced with a strong dose of amnesia. The mythical good old days never did exist, of course, not even in football. But this is precisely why the evocation of a supposedly pure and original form of the game is so significant and appealing. Even the BBC markets a 1970s football highlights DVD as a flashback to 'football's golden era'. The decade was so golden that England failed to qualify for the World Cup finals twice in a row.

Over the coming years English (club) football will nonetheless remain the most successful in the world, if only on account of the viewing figures. There is scarcely any other entertainment product that offers so much honest, authentic emotion, as well as reference points to a class consciousness that vanished in Germany and most other places decades ago. To look at England, therefore, is also to look at an unadulterated version of the game, one that is still deeply connected to its social roots – in the imagination of the viewing public at least.

It may also be true that the modern world loves English football because it recognises it as an idealised version of itself. Space and time are extremely limited, the competition tough, the crazed acceleration of everything takes your breath away, yet the noble principle of fairness ensures that nobody breaks the rules and that, at the end, the game is only won by those who deserve it.

CHAPTER 1

Take It Like a Man: The Pleasure of Suffering

It had to begin down the pub. On 26 October 1863 representatives from seven football teams met in the Freemasons Tavern in Great Queen Street, London, to establish an association and unify the rules. On 8 December – after six meetings, countless beers, minor scuffles and an unsuccessful rebellion – the newly founded Football Association (FA) issued the rules which were henceforth binding. The sport proceeded to conquer the entire country and travelled 'on the wings of the British Empire', as the sociologist John Sugden puts it, until it had reached every corner of the world.

So much we already know. When referring to England, German sports reporters, forever searching for epithets, do not have to strain too hard. They write *Mutterland des Fussballs* ('motherland of football'), or 'cradle of football', and everybody understands. But do they? These stock phrases only ring true at first glance. Although England has a lot to do with the history of football, the game originates from somewhere else. Football, or *Tsu-Chu*, as one should call it (*Tsu* means 'kick', *Chu*, 'the ball'), was played in China by soldiers of the Tsin dynasty as far back as the third century BC. So football was certainly not born, as the words 'mother' and 'cradle' suggest, in Britain. But it was raised here, and here it went to school – to a strict 'public school', to be precise. This particular education made the game what it is today.

To German ears, 'public school' is a complete misnomer. It's really the opposite of what it says: not a public educational institution, financed by the state, but a private school, a boarding school originally established for the scions of the upper class. Eton, the most famous of all public schools, currently asks for around £8,000 to educate each of its boys – per term, of course. Public schools are not for the public at large. These institutions do like the term, however, because it elegantly obscures the actual scheme of things. This is hardly a coincidence. Whenever the somewhat uncomfortable subject of class differences comes up in England, obscurantist word play and euphemisms become very popular. It's the classic British trick of understatement.

In their endeavours to imitate the nobility, on the other hand, the middle and working classes are only too eager to claim aristocratic terminology as their own. Thus vile tower blocks from the post-war era are called 'courts'. Victorian 'mansions' are not villas on the edge of town but apartment blocks. And the plebeian origins of football also manifest themselves in the deliberately confused, upwardly mobile terminology the sport itself uses: in England the old Second Division is now grandiloquently called the 'Championship', the Third is 'League One', and the Fourth is 'League Two'.

Curiously, however, when it came to the development of the game, things worked the other way round. In the middle of the nineteenth century the social elite suddenly aped the masses and discovered the round piece of leather for themselves. Until that time, it's fair to say that football was not really a sport in Britain, merely a decent excuse for drunkenness, mass punch-ups, wanton property damage and the bloody settling of old feuds. Several kings attempted in vain to prohibit these ancient battles for the ball between villages and towns that were played out in woods and meadows.

At the time many public schools had serious problems with discipline. There was little money; the boys were always rebelling and beating each other up. Consequently one of the most renowned boarding schools, Harrow, had only sixty-nine pupils in 1844. A succession of young, pious headmasters recognised the problem and prescribed all sorts of physical exercise for their protégés. The clergy saw themselves as 'muscular Christians'. They rejected the Church's traditional negative attitude towards the physical and insisted that the exercising of the body should go hand in hand with the boys' intellectual and spiritual education. Already in the 1820s and 1830s Dr Thomas Arnold, headmaster at Rugby, encouraged his pupils to play a form of football. (According to legend, it was at Rugby in 1823 that William Webb Ellis, a boy from Manchester, caught the ball during a match and, contrary to all conventions, ran with it under his arm towards the opposition goal line. This was the start of rugby football, about which more later.)

Arnold was the most influential pedagogue of the Victorian era. But for the development of, and long-term influence on, football the key figures were the Thring brothers. Reverend Edward Thring, the older of the two, turned the relatively obscure Uppingham School into one of the most popular institutions in Britain after he became headmaster in 1853. Under his revolutionary leadership it became a leading sports school. Football and cricket were organised as compulsory subjects. Thring himself joined in with enthusiasm. This muscular Christian was convinced that sport would make 'men out of weaklings', moreover that it could distract adolescent boys from 'antisocial or even disgusting personal activities', as Hunter Davies writes in *Boots, Balls and Haircuts.* And there was one thing above all others that the Victorians understood by 'disgusting personal activities': masturbation.

Thring swore to combat this 'abominable sin'; he was convinced it led straight to an 'early and dishonourable grave'. To vouchsafe the purity of his institution, Thring encouraged the boys to spy on one another. 'Self-abuse' led to an immediate expulsion from the school.

In his brilliant book *Those Feet,* a journey through the cultural peculiarities of English football, David Winner shows that Thring's odd anxieties were shared by society at the time. 'Victorian England was assailed by many sexual terrors. Prostitution, syphilis, the so-called "white slave trade" and homosexuality were all seen as great moral and social evils. But masturbation was somehow thought to underlie all of them.' Sport emerged as the most important vehicle for preventing auto-sexual activity; and also became a social code that directed young Englishmen towards masculinity, conformity and militarism. The new imperial age could make good use of such seasoned young men. 'The masturbation panic was so ubiquitous there was a strong emphasis against solitude, against privacy and against individualism,' the historian Katy Mullin writes. 'Team sports, football in particular, were brought in as an antidote. It was to stop solipsism.'

J. C. Thring, at the time a student in Cambridge, had quite different concerns. He had played football at Shrewsbury School, but now could seldom organise matches because the boys were used to completely different sets of rules from their own public schools. Thus in 1862 the younger Thring brother wrote *The Simplest Game,* a pamphlet with ten simple rules. These were posted around Parker's Piece, Cambridge's sports ground. In the north of England, where in 1857 Sheffield United had been founded as the first football club in the world, few people took any notice initially. Yet the need to codify football once and for all continued to grow, and led to the aforementioned meeting in Covent Garden's Freemasons Tavern. Eton, Harrow, Winchester, Rugby and Westminster boycotted the meeting outright. They would not accept any interference.

The founding fathers did not allow the rebels to ruffle them. The discussion only became heated when the controversial issue of 'hacking' came up – the deliberate kicking of another player's shins. The battle lines were soon drawn. For Mr F. W. Campbell, the representative of Blackheath Football Club, football without hacking was a thing for soft men 'who liked their pipes and grog or schnaps more than the manly game'. J. C. Thring could not let this criticism pass. 'Football, by its very nature, is rough enough, and cannot be effeminate,' he said. Deliberate hacking, however, was neither fair nor manly, 'but thoroughly barbaric, and un-English'. Campbell, the dedicated hard man, maintained the opposite was true: 'If you do away with [hacking], you will do away with all the courage and pluck of the game, and I will be bound to bring over a lot of Frenchmen who would beat you with a week's practice.' The insult struck a chord, but was not enough to win the argument for Campbell. He lost the vote. When the new FA also banned players from running with the ball under their arm, Blackheath left the association in protest. From that point on there were two football camps: Association football, or soccer to give it its common name, and rugby football. Much to Mr Campbell's chagrin, however, hacking was also forbidden in the laws of rugby, issued in 1871.

The hacking issue is more than just an amusing anecdote, as it poses the key question of English football, the one that covertly dominates all others: are you hard enough, or just a schnapps-drinking, pipe-smoking Frenchman?

Every match is played out in the great shadow of this fundamental criterion. Every player who steps on to the turf has to defend himself against the ancient accusation of being too soft. What makes his task more difficult is that, since its birth, football has been on the defensive in this respect: those who play rugby, their arch-rivals, are patently the harder, manlier sportsmen. Therefore, English football has always tended to over-compensate and err on the side of violence. Countless continental opponents would routinely complain that their English counterparts were behaving like rugby players on the pitch – and they were right, of course, more than they knew. However much the game in Britain may have changed over the last ten years with the mass influx of foreign players and managers, the hardness gene in the DNA of English football has proved extremely resistant. The rough approach is still its defining characteristic.

For most foreigners the first few weeks in the Premier League are a culture shock. After his transfer from Marseille in 2000, it famously took Frenchman Robert Pires six months to get used to the 'rugby-like tackles'. Five years later he could still occasionally be seen shaking his head after escaping yet another homicidal attack in the centre circle – of course the referee had waved play on. In England, the rules are the same but interpreted very differently from elsewhere; even the most vicious attack seems excusable if the ball was somewhere in the vicinity. After the leg is broken or the skull smashed in, the intentions of the defender are always construed as generously as possible. 'He meant to play the ball,' referees and commentators say, nodding their heads in agreement.

When Reading's Stephen Hunt nearly killed Chelsea keeper Petr Cech in October 2006, BBC pundit Mark Lawrenson dismissed it as 'a clumsy challenge, if anything'. He had 'had the right' to challenge the keeper for the loose ball, said Lawrenson. Since Hunt had not injured Cech intentionally, it could only have been an unfortunate accident. No one realised grievous bodily harm can also be caused by gross negligence or recklessness. 'If goalkeepers will not be better protected, one of us will end up in a wheelchair before too long,' Arsenal stopper Jens Lehmann warned at the time. Naturally he was dismissed as a continental crank.

Two years after the Cech incident, Arsenal striker Eduardo had his shin, fibula and ankle broken by Birmingham defender Martin Taylor. The foul was so gruesome that Sky refused to show a repeat. 'I've never seen a worse injury in thirteen years,' said the programme director Grant Best. Football's reaction, though, was depressingly familiar. 'Martin's not that type of player,' said Birmingham manager Alex McLeish. 'It's not in his make-up to produce a malicious tackle.' On *Match of the Day*, Lawrenson thought it had been – wait for it – 'a clumsy tackle'. There is a sense that this kind of collateral damage is sadly inevitable if English football is not to become too soft. It was left to Arsène Wenger to attack the institutional brutality of the game. 'We always hear "he is not the type for a bad foul" or other nonsense,' he said, 'but a murderer only has to kill once.' Wenger's understandable outburst caused more upset than Taylor's horror-tackle. Tellingly, Alan Hansen saved his harshest words for Arsenal captain William Gallas, who had sat down on the pitch and shed a few tears in Birmingham. 'That's not professional,' sneered the BBC expert.

The fourteenth of August 2005, Highbury. A typical scene. Newcastle United's Jermaine Jenas, not exactly known for being a thug, tackles Arsenal's Gilberto Silva from behind near the halfway line. Jenas's left leg just touches the ball, but he also thrusts in his right leg with all his might. The Brazilian is almost cut in half. Referee Steve Bennett is standing only a few yards away and shows the red card for excessive force. Andy Gray, one of the Sky commentators and the most esteemed expert in the country, cannot believe it. 'But he was clearly playing the ball! A shocking decision, a disgrace.' United's manager, Graeme Souness, only saw a 'hard tackle' as well, and for days afterwards a storm of indignation rages through the papers. Even the liberal *Guardian* thinks a booking would have sufficed. Because of the media response, Bennett starts to have doubts about his decision. Although the slow-motion replays confirm his original verdict, the day after the match he asks the Football Association to change the red card to a yellow one. 'Steve Bennett has written a letter to Graeme Souness, Jermaine Jenas and the rest of the team, apologising for his erroneous decision,' a Newcastle spokesman announces. The FA agrees to the request. Football is still a man's game; everybody is happy. Apart from Arsène Wenger. But then again, the Arsenal manager *is*, of course, a Frenchman.

Belatedly, the more enlightened section of the English media has begun to face up to the problem. 'Anyone who denies that we have an endemic problem with high, wide and late potentially limb-snapping "challenges" should be excluded right away from the debate,' Paul Hayward wrote in the *Observer* in March 2009, after a particularly nasty round of midweek matches. NIGHT OF SHAME! BONE-CRUNCHING STARS DARKEN THE PREMIER LEAGUE was the *Daily Mail's* take, and the *News of the World* asked for two of the perpetrators to be put in 'handcuffs' – interestingly, not because of the violence as such but the 'disrespect to authority'. Once again it was left to Wenger to explain to the locals the difference between a perfectly good tackle, designed to win the ball, and 'jumping in like a mad guy, where you can destroy the legs of anybody'.

In 2006 the Alsatian had considered taking legal action against Sunderland's Dan Smith when his challenge left Abou Diaby with a broken leg and a dislocated ankle.

Wenger's Gunners precisely straddle the fault-line of this and many other debates about the changing nature of England's game. They are the most obvious example of just how the sport has evolved, yet how doggedly it has remained true to its own ideals. On a good day, the game played by Wenger's multinational squad of technicians transcended English football altogether. For many years their winning combination of unbelievable pace and skill knew no peers. Like an acclaimed master artist who at the height of his creative power has overcome all self-doubt, and who is totally aware of the greatness of his art, Arsenal could be sure that the beautiful flashes of inspiration would appear at some point. The pitch at Highbury (and later, on occasions, at the Emirates Stadium) became a canvas on which complicated patterns of geometric lines would come together in master-pieces of the avant-garde. The enigmatic runs and flowing, direct passes – the North Londoners operated entirely without crosses or long balls – were too much for Arsenal's opponents. In the 2003–04 season they went undefeated playing this magical brand of football. Yet, while the newspapers went head over heels in their praise for the 'Invincibles', you could sense that the English somehow found the success of this team unsettling. Individuals who used their brains this much in football, the unspoken suspicion went, probably did so because they lacked the courage for real battle.

This crude prejudice seemed to be confirmed whenever Arsenal encountered their rivals Manchester United. Alex Ferguson's team play a wonderfully fluid attacking football of their own making these days. But in the 'Djemba-Djemba years' (Matt Dickinson in *The Times*), when the Gunners set the pace, United often fought them with a primitive English hardness bordering on brutality. In October 2004 it was ironically at Old Trafford that Arsenal's run of forty-nine games without a defeat came to an end, after the cultured souls from north London were thoroughly kicked off the pitch by United's street-fighters. Wenger complained that his players had not been sufficiently protected by the referee; for this he was labelled a whinger. 'The modern game has turned us into hypocrites,' wrote Rob Bagchi in the *Guardian*. 'We profess to prefer silky skills but when our team is fannying about it doesn't take long for even the aesthetes to yell "get stuck in" if not the more chilling "get some blood on your boots" that used to be a regular staple at grounds a couple of decades ago.'

Mr Campbell, the hacking advocate, would surely have enjoyed the occasion in September 2005 when the former United player, Phil Neville – now in the services of Everton – gave Robert Pires a deliberate whack in the thigh without being punished by the referee. The ball, it is true, had not been far away. 'He aimed at me and he hit me,' said the Frenchman, who had to be substituted after the incident. Neville gave a typically English response: 'Robert Pires is an absolutely fantastic player who has put in some unbelievable performances since he has come to this country. But in English football, you have got to tackle. Sometimes when you play against these type of players, it's as if they have it in their contracts that you are not allowed to tackle them. Well, Everton's strength and my strength is tackling and it may be a more British type of game.'

In English football mythology, the place of honour which elsewhere is taken by brilliant ball conjurors or super-technicians is often reserved for the hard men: defensive midfielders or defenders who tackle their opponents into the ground. According to a 2004 survey, Roy Keane, Manchester United's Irish firebrand, was the hardest of the hard lads. In April 2001 he kicked the Norwegian Alf Inge Haaland (Manchester City) in the kneecap – deliberately. 'I waited until five minutes before the end,' he writes in his autobiography. 'I gave it to him fucking hard. I think the ball was nearby. Take that, you cunt!' Charming.

In second place: Ron 'Chopper' Harris, Chelsea captain and pantomime villain of the 1960s and 1970s. A few minutes into the 1970 Cup final replay against Leeds United, Harris's outstretched leg smashed into Eddie Gray's pelvis. Deliberate assault? Play on – no yellow card. Harris's karate kick made history; it was the most famous foul in the dirtiest game of all time. At the time Leeds had a large contingent of scrappers in its ranks, including Johnny Giles, Billy Bremner and Norman 'Bite yer legs' Hunter. Fists were flying all over the place on the pitch. But in the end Chelsea won 2–1, thereby winning the FA Cup for the first time.

At the end of the 1990s, Premier League referee David Elleray watched a video recording of that final. He came to the conclusion that, using today's interpretation of the rules, there would have been twenty yellow cards and six sendings-off.

Third in the survey was Vinnie Jones, who took such care to nurture his bad-guy image that after his career finished he was able to reprise the role in Hollywood films such as *Gone in Sixty Seconds* and *Swordfish*. As Wimbledon captain in the late 1980s the Welshman radiated fear and dread. His record? Thirteen red cards. His victims included Paul Gascoigne (grabbing his privates – the notorious 'wedding tackle') and Kenny Dalglish (Liverpool). Before the 1988 FA Cup final Jones had threatened to rip off the Scot's ear and then 'spit in the hole'. The London kick-and-rush mob pulled off a complete surprise with a 1–0 victory. Four years later Jones brought out the video *Soccer's Hard Men*, which glorified the most blatant rule-breaking antics of Bremner and co. and gave practical tips for copying them. 'The best thing is to kick him in the Achilles' heel,' Jones informed the audience. 'If you're smart, the ref won't see it.' The FA was outraged. Jones was hit with a £20,000 fine for 'bringing football into disrepute'.

For the most part, England's admiration for these axe-men is not entirely earnest. Hard men are also popularly known as 'hard nuts'. Anti-heroes, these are the types who bully younger pupils in the playground. They are the sort of blokes mothers warn their daughters about. They breach the rules of fair play just a touch too blatantly to be considered proper role models. People find them fascinating, but are happy to be quite normal by comparison.

In theory, everyone can dish it out. But ultimately it is a different type of violence that English football demands from its protagonists. The law of the pitch is: it is more blessed to receive than give. As the motto goes: 'Take it like a man.' That sounds like a contradiction, but not for Englishmen. Being a real man means first and foremost being able to take it.

Traditionally, the ability to grin and bear it has been the decisive trait of the English upper class. A popular maxim in public schools was that it was a good thrashing which made real gentlemen out of young men. It was dealt out most severely at Eton. Reverend Dr John Keate used to beat on average ten boys a day, only taking a break on Sundays. On 30 June 1832 he surpassed himself: eighty boys had their backsides spanked. When the headmaster had completed his work, the boys applauded him for his stamina.

The notion of the 'stiff upper lip' represents the ideal mode of behaviour according to which the Englishman must suffer everything without losing his composure. This stoical approach to life adopted by Her Majesty's subjects perhaps explains the catastrophic state of health care and public transport. People take pride in getting on with it. A 'lack of temperament', on the other hand, is unforgivable. By this the English do not mean blandness, but poor control over one's own emotions. He who does not bear his suffering quietly and is easily provoked into a careless reaction fails as an Englishman and as a man. In no other country would David Beckham have been branded a national traitor after his revenge foul against the Argentinian Diego Simeone at the 1998 World Cup, essentially harmless, brought him a red card. The huge admiration felt for Gary Lineker, on the other hand, stems from the fact that he was not booked once throughout his career. Not because he was a meek goody-two-shoes, but because he was someone who could take it and never retaliate.

Self-control is also a must in moments of joy. As late as the 1960s, the customary way of celebrating a goal in the First Division was with a firm handshake. When the players followed the bad example of foreigners and started to hug, even kiss, one another, the FA was not very amused. 'It is to be hoped that this theatrical affectation is just a passing phase,' ran an official statement from the late 1970s.

One of football's key selling points is the passion it generates. English football has never forgotten that passion comes from the Latin *passio* (suffering, enduring). It's impossible to overstate the importance of this quasi-religious concept. Writing in *Süddeutsche Zeitung* about the fiftieth anniversary of the Munich air disaster, I could not help but notice that 'in Protestant Britain, heroes are not measured by the greatness of their deeds, only by the greatness of their suffering'. Part of the hostility towards Manchester United seems motivated by a perverse sense of envy from rival supporters: no other club can match United's tragedy.

In Liverpool, the victims of Hillsborough are glorified as martyrs for the red cause. The club has found a strange kind of redemption in their needless deaths. Their blood has washed the sins of Heysel away.

Pick up a newspaper, and you will find that everybody who has endured a grave loss or suffers from an affliction is described as 'brave'. Convention demands it, irrespective of the circumstances. Nothing validates you like terminal illness. *Big Brother* 'star' Jade Goody had disgraced herself with racist comments. Cancer allowed her to be reborn, before death, as a veritable saint. The more she suffered, the more the nation took her to heart.

In a culture that places so much value on suffering, the line between pain and pleasure is not always clearly defined. In the few remaining red telephone boxes in London one is confronted by an assortment of brightly coloured cards with women's telephone numbers, offering spanking to their customers. Hundreds of grown-up men turn up dressed in school uniforms to fetish parties every weekend to be spanked by women. Why? In David Winner's *Those Feet*, a banker and fan of spanking explains that 'whenever my father used to beat me, he insisted that I kept a straight face and didn't cry. If I managed this, he would congratulate me. Psychologists say that this is why I associate pain with love and respect.'

When the Manchester United fan Robbie Williams released his 2001 album of Broadway classics *Swing When You're Winning*, he was asked in an interview by *Der Spiegel* what he admired most about his idols Frank Sinatra and Dean Martin. 'The way they held a drink,' was the reply from the former Take That member. The German magazine misinterpreted the answer, believing that Williams was referring to the Rat Pack's elegant manner, not their fabled ability to get plastered. Being able to hold alcohol in one's body belongs to the art form of 'taking it'. The proverbial piss-ups in Britain are a sort of liquid spanking – an internal torture. A form of pleasurable suffering and an initiation: it separates the men from the boys.

An English footballer was supposed to be able to drink; there was no getting round that. In the 1960s and 1970s whole careers were pissed up the wall, including that of George Best. When Alex Ferguson became manager of Manchester United in 1986 he discovered he was in charge of a regally paid pub team. Centred around the leader Bryan Robson, the lads used to go on a bender after every training session. United might have been an extreme case, but the practice was very common at the time. 'The foreign players don't go out drinking with the other lads,' complained Harry Redknapp as recently as the mid-1990s, when he was in charge at West Ham.

Among the working class, who were so important in the development of football, the very same rules of toughness apply, albeit for other reasons originally. For those nineteenth-century men living and working in inhumane conditions, resilience and hardness were not abstract values but qualities necessary for survival: there was no other way to overcome the squalor. This specifically accentuated version of masculinity combined with the Protestant ethic (work, deprivation and renunciation) to produce a powerful ideology which suited the moneyed classes.

The Christian pioneers of football had a formidable sense of mission. They had a staunch belief in the moral potential of sport and energetically supported its distribution throughout the working class. Famous clubs such as Aston Villa, Liverpool, Everton, Birmingham City, Bolton Wanderers, Manchester City, Fulham and Southampton were founded as clergy teams. The preachers themselves thought nothing of getting their own socks dirty. Arthur Kinnaird, Old Etonian and son of the lady who founded the

Young Women's Christian Association (YWCA), became the sport's first star with nine Cup final appearances in the 1870s and 1880s. This tall, red-bearded man was notorious for his fearless tackles and unreserved commitment. 'I fear he will come home one day with a broken leg,' his anxious mother told the FA president Sir Francis Marindin. 'Do not worry,' Sir Francis replied, 'it will not be one of his own.' Kinnaird later became president of the FA, and during his thirty-three years in office found the time to involve himself in the 'Pure Literary Society', an association for pure, morally irreproachable writing. 'Football and purity were not merely ideologically connected: they also shared personnel,' Winner writes.

Even harder than Kinnaird was E. C. Bambridge, a player for the Corinthians. Even after the admission of professional footballers in 1885 the Corinthians remained committed amateurs and were able to put up with quite a lot. Bambridge's courage was 'legendary', as it says in B. O. Corbett's book *The Annals of the Corinthian Football Club*, published in 1906. A broken leg had forced Bambridge to spend a long time on the sidelines, but he desperately wanted to play in an important match even though the bone had not fully mended. He tied a white shin pad over his sock. At half-time blood was seeping out from underneath it: his opponents had been kicking him deliberately. But Bambridge hung on and in the second half scored the winning goal. After the match he took off the shin pad and revealed to his team-mates that he had tied it around the leg that was fine. His injured leg had been unprotected but remained untouched.

In the English sense of the word, however, probably the most heroic performance of all time was by a German, of all people. Bernd 'Bert' Trautmann, born in Bremen, had stayed in Britain after being a prisoner of war, and became

Manchester City's goalkeeper. Fifteen minutes before the end of the 1956 Cup final he collided with a Birmingham City attacker. When he came round he stayed in goal, despite serious pains in his neck, and with some excellent saves helped City to a 3–1 victory. Three days later he was diagnosed in hospital with a broken vertebra in the neck. The 137-year history of the Cup is brimming with wonderful goals and fantastic achievements, but it would be impossible to find a more glorious example of self-sacrifice. It is interesting to note that after the 2005 Champions League final in Istanbul, Dietmar Hamann was praised by the newspapers chiefly for the fact that he had bravely played on with a broken metatarsus and converted his penalty. The strategic change in Liverpool's fortunes brought about by his coming on as a substitute for the second half was largely overlooked.

This glorification of tough men can also be traced back to the sport's rules. As substitutions were not permitted until 1965, tough players who did not feel pain were particularly valuable in a league where one's physical integrity was under threat at all times. The referees seldom intervened, as men were expected to look after themselves. Few matches finished with twenty-two fit players on the pitch. The only players to drop out were those who could no longer walk unassisted. Foreigners lying on the touchline are still astounded today by just how quickly some team doctors send them back on to the pitch to 'run off' their injury. 'Run it off, son!' they shout. The idea must be that a player can run away from the pain so long as he has the necessary courage.

The 'blood, sweat and tears' mentality that is so deeply anchored in the genetic make-up of English football has allowed the emergence of certain types of player, while simultaneously making it very difficult for cultured technicians to survive in the game. Usually on islands you tend to find rare species which, due to a lack of natural predators, have become widespread and have not had to develop flight or defence behaviour mechanisms. In the English football biotope, on the other hand, the evolution of the sport has produced so many 'hard dogs' that the few birds of paradise have always faced an acute threat of extinction.

Before examining the tragic fate of these 'un-English' players in more detail, you have to admit here that the players' ability to 'take it' provides a not insignificant chunk of English football's unique charm. We are not talking about the voyeuristic delight in seeing iron studs tear into opponents' calves, but about a way of playing the game that is naturally open and attractive in its ideal form. How well do hardness and the attacking spirit go together? They can actually complement each other very well, as a glance at the natural counterpart and *bête noire* of the Premier League, the Italian Serie A, proves.

In the Italian league the infamously destructive tactics of *catenaccio* (the bolt or chain) are generally accepted as a legitimate means of winning. Why? Or, to put it differently, why was it that Italy developed such a style of play? One must be wary of clichés, but clean-sheet football seems, on the face of it, unbefitting of a culture that values beauty and sensual pleasures. But perhaps it does fit exactly with the psychology of the players, with their machismo? Could it be that the worst fear of an Italian – after losing the love of his mother – was to have 'one slipped in', in other words to be turned into a woman by his opponents? If so, then this could explain why preventing a goal was seen as more important than scoring oneself.

The English male, by contrast, as we have already seen, is defined by his ability to take it. Anybody too concerned with protecting his own goal cannot be considered clever, but a coward. People want to see cavalier football. We are not talking about gentlemanly acts of courtesy on the pitch here, but matches in which the teams go at each other like fearless duellers without any regard for possible losses.

A true Englishman is not afraid of setbacks. Subconsciously he even yearns for them, as true greatness only manifests itself in moments of maximum adversity. This is the bulldog spirit. A victory in an apparently hopeless cause is more honourable than one where the opponent is thrashed 5–0. Only losses and pain make victory a real pleasure. It is not sadism that drives on the English footballer, but masochism. Eamon Dunphy, a Second Division player with Millwall in the 1970s, writes in his diary *Only a Game?*, 'The lads know, especially in the lower divisions, that the one thing that keeps them in the game is their application. Their dedication. The intensity with which they approach the game. Which leads them to this feeling that they have got to go out and punish themselves for ninety minutes. This is crucial to players, particularly in the lower divisions. It is one of the most important things in the game at the moment – the idea that you somehow have to suffer.' The same is true for those watching the game. 'Nick Hornby's *Fever Pitch* encapsulated it perfectly,' the football academic John Williams says. 'More than anything else, to be a fan is to suffer.'

There's this idea gaining ground in Germany, the view that you can only claim to be a true fan after having attended your thousandth away game, bare-chested in deepest Siberia. Ideally, you will have sold one of your kidneys to fund the twenty-seven-hour round trip. It is a notion imported from England, of course, and it is Protestant through and through. It betrays the bad conscience of the total fan: he justifies his pleasure by masking it as pain and hard work.

Fun in the stadium? No thanks, we're English. There have

even been warnings against good football. 'Watching these two might give people a taste for it and could be damaging for football in our country,' cautioned Cliff Lloyd, the secretary of the players' union, in summer 1978 after Tottenham had signed the Argentinian world champions Osvaldo 'Ossie' Ardiles and Ricardo 'Ricky' Villa. Unthinkable to let such artists near the ball; where would it leave the English game? Where the Premier League is today, with its array of superstars.

The fiction of martyrdom must nevertheless be preserved, especially since the grounds have become ever more comfortable. If the game is supposed to be an ordeal then the supporters must suffer as well, in order that they can belong.

If you ask fans about their favourite matches they talk about famous victories against local rivals (especially away wins) and finals. One motif comes up again and again: the team secured their triumph 'against all odds'.

'For me the best game was the 1991 Cup final against Nottingham Forest,' says Spurs fan Ben Lyttleton. 'In his last game for us Paul Gascoigne was so badly injured in the first few minutes that he had to come off. Then Stuart Pearce made it 1–0 to Nottingham Forest. Gary Lineker had a goal disallowed for us because he was wrongly adjudged offside. Later he missed a penalty. We thought that the game was over at that point. But then we managed to equalise, and in extra-time a Forest defender put it into his own goal and we won the Cup.'

The Gunner Marc Fels recalls most fondly Arsenal's victory at Anfield on the last day of the 1988–89 season. 'We were leading 1–0, but needed to win 2–0 to become champions, because Liverpool had the better goal difference. We're in the ninety-first minute and no one thinks we can do it any more. The Liverpool players are getting ready to celebrate. Then

Micky Thomas takes the ball in midfield, beats three Reds and smashes the ball in. Champions!'

'I can think of two games,' says Sunderland fan Jonathan Wilson. 'One, a 2–1 victory over Chelsea in the 1992 Cup semi-final. We equalised in the eighty-sixth minute to make it 1–1, but we were convinced we didn't have a chance in extra-time, because Chelsea had played us into the ground. But two minutes later Gordon Armstrong headed in a goal from sixteen yards. The other match was a 3–2 victory against Manchester United, in November 1984. We were trailing 2–0, but then Clive Walker scored a hat-trick.'

Manchester United supporters reserve their greatest affection for the 2–1 victory against Bayern Munich in Barcelona in 1999 (two goals in the last minute). Scousers get goose pimples at the mention of the Champions League final against AC Milan in Istanbul: '3–0 down at half-time and we still won – it doesn't get better than that,' says John Williams, a fan of the Reds. In the vocabulary of English football there is a very interesting expression for such unexpected comebacks: coming from behind. It may be that the double entendre here is not entirely a coincidence. Williams says, 'Screwing is more fun if you've been screwed before.' Which brings us back to pleasurable pain. And sex.

Let us recall the Reverend Edward Thring and the Victorian fear of masturbation. In *Those Feet*, David Winner argues that the ideal rules of behaviour established by football's founding fathers prescribed an 'asexual physicality', a masculinity that deliberately rejected any form of sensuality. The only aesthetic permitted was that of the honourable fight. For Winner, the failure of 'sensual' players with a love of the ball is the tragic consequence of the hostility to pleasure codified in the sport from the start: football must not be sexy.

The Dutch, inspired as they are by the spirit of footballing beauty, see things very differently of course. During the 1996 European Championship, Ruud Gullit in the BBC television studio praised the sexy football of the Portuguese national side. The venerable presenter Des Lynam, the housewives' favourite, raised his eyebrows in astonishment. In thirty-five years of reporting on football, the man with the grey moustache had never heard anything like it. 'Football is at its best when it's sexy,' Gullit explained, 'when it's creative. When the players give free rein to their imagination and their natural skills. When they enjoy it and it's fun to watch.' This moment has entered into English television football history, because it broke a taboo. Clearly, the sensual dimension of the sport had never been discussed so openly before. Typically, it had to be a foreigner who did it.

'Why don't the English play sexy football?' Winner asks. 'The answer, in part at least, is that the very idea of sexy football transgresses one of the English game's most sacred founding principles.' Football, in other words, is the opposite of sex. Sexual repression.

But is that really true? Take a look at a former British colony and quite the opposite interpretation suggests itself. For decades people have been puzzled as to why football has never been able to establish itself in the USA. Some say that there are simply not enough goals during the matches. After all, Americans love nothing more than success, and in football this occurs rather too infrequently. So rarely, in fact, that sometimes there is no success at all. That surely isn't right. No wonder that for a long time in Major League soccer draws were not permitted. A penalty shoot-out decided the game and guaranteed that the ball made its way into the net at least a few times. 'In America, everybody wants to have dessert first,' Jack White of the rock band the White Stripes once told me.

In comparison with American football, soccer is simply too soft, another argument goes. It is endlessly derided as a girls' sport and this puts off the natural target group of young men. It sounds plausible, but neglects the fact that 'soccer' has become hugely popular at amateur level for boys, too, in recent years.

Perhaps there is a third, far less obvious explanation. Might it be that a sport that sees two teams trying to slip one in on each other just has too many sexual undertones for American tastes? There can be no doubt that the general public in the USA is much more puritanical than in the rest of the Western world. When Janet Jackson's bare nipple flickered on television screens for a few seconds during the half-time show at Superbowl XXXVIII (2004), half the nation took to the barricades. Moral indignation knew no bounds. (In English stadiums, by contrast, every streaker, be they a man or a woman, is greeted with warm applause.)

The metaphorical connection between sex and scoring a goal can also not easily be dismissed, even if it rarely manifests itself so candidly as in the goal-scorer's insistence that putting the ball in the net felt 'better than an orgasm'. 'The goalkeeper who has a ball shot past him would never describe the experience as an exhilarating act of copulation,' writes Dirk Schümer, journalist for the *Frankfurter Allgemeine Zeitung*. 'Although football is like sex, it is only so for one party. Gratification comes as a ballistic masterstroke which the opponents experience as rape.' It can never be proved empirically, but there's the suspicion that the prudish Americans are subconsciously troubled by all the meta-phorical sexual intercourse they're witnessing on the pitch. Football might be too immoral for them, the sexual subtext a touch too explicit. The American public does not want to watch men trying to screw each other on prime-time.

'But American football can be deconstructed in exactly the same way,' John Williams argues. 'After all, the aim is to break the opponents' resistance and to get the ball into their endzone.' Quite. Yet the symbolism of football is that much more pronounced, starting with the very mechanics of the sport: the aim of the game is to shoot, thrust or shove something small and white into an opening. It doesn't need the genius of Sigmund Freud to work out what is being simulated here. Derek Hammond takes a similar view. The origins of football go back to ancient fertility rituals, the historian argues in Winner's book. 'These are pre-Christian, pagan rituals which only survived because they were in places everyone forgot about. They were probably part of the original heathen, naturalistic British religions which were about the earth and the sun, and killing and fucking.'

The pious Thring brothers may not have known that. Football, which they promoted as an instrument of physical and spiritual chastisement, was probably so successful due to a crass error in the system: the sexual energy of young men was not suppressed on the pitch as intended, but perfectly sublimated. Scoring goals: a clean form of hormonal discharge.

The founding fathers were able to control a football discourse kept strictly within the limits of asexual masculinity, but not the players' feelings. Everyday language reveals that footballers have an instinctive grasp of the secret connection between their sport and sex, and that they see through their own game. Take the verb 'to score'. It initially described a purely administrative activity: after a goal, a notch was carved into the post to keep a record of the state of play. Over time the term came to describe the feat of shooting the ball between the posts. But to score is also, of course, a vernacular expression for sex. In the film of Irvine Welsh's novel

Trainspotting a sex scene alternated with a recording of Archie Gemmill's famous goal for Scotland at the 1978 World Cup. 'I haven't felt that good since Archie Gemmill scored against Holland,' Ewan McGregor says after his orgasm. The collected anecdotes of playboy George Best are entitled *Scoring at Half-Time*, which has nothing to do with goals during the interval.

The fact that 34 per cent of the 1,900 men polled by mycelebrityfashion.co.uk in 2009 preferred their wives or girlfriends to wear shirts of their favourite football (or rugby) club in bed tells you everything about the surreptitious sexual allure of the beautiful game, even if it manifests itself in that typically English, jokey and somewhat repressed fashion.

Opposition strikers who fail to score are taunted from the stands by refrains of 'He couldn't score in a brothel!', sung to the tune of 'Guantanamera'. After Wayne Rooney's indiscretion in a Liverpool 'massage parlour' they sang 'You only score in a brothel!' Quite often a manager will shout 'Up his arse!' to one of his defenders if he is standing too far away from an opponent. And even the hardest, straightest blokes, those beyond any suspicion, will occasionally admit to their mates that they 'creamed their pants' after scoring or witnessing a great goal.

Professional football restrains itself from such crass salaciousness out of consideration for younger TV viewers. When Arsenal play, Sky coyly displays the strange abbreviation 'ASNL' in the right-hand corner of the screen, 'ARS' or 'ARSE' presumably bringing to mind too readily the word for the human posterior.

By contrast, the highbrow, left-leaning German broadsheet *taz* appreciated goal-keeping legend Oliver Kahn as 'an aesthete of the anal' whose one and only concern was to make sure that 'nothing came in at the back'. Taking their cue from Schümer, *taz* realised that Kahn never enjoyed 'the striker's orgasmic joy at scoring' – because he knew he was the one getting shafted. 'I'm the arse,' Kahn once said about conceding a goal: 'a feeling of loneliness grabs hold of me'. Who but a certified maniac would want to engage in such an existentialist fight against the odds?

In an interview to promote his book *Ich: Erfolg kommt von innen* (*I: Success Comes from the Inside*), Kahn cited Rambo and eighties soap *Dallas* as an inspiration. Winning was his dream, very early on. As a six-year-old, Kahn's hero was Scrooge McDuck. He bought a walking stick with his pocket money and instructed his mum to fill up the bathtub with coins. 'A classic case for child counselling,' wrote *Der Spiegel*. Instead he went into goal, where many similarly deranged young Germans have traditionally found refuge.

Germany's unique obsession with big, strong, mad keepers can be traced back to the 3–2 win over Hungary in the World Cup final of 1954, when radio reporter Herbert Zimmermann praised keeper Toni Turek as a *Fussballgott* (football god). After the catastrophe of the Second World War, the sort of nationalistic fervour and sense of supremacy that sporting success brings in its wake was widely seen as unacceptable. Consequently, the natural admiration for strikers – in Schümer's terms the men entrusted to screw the opposition – shifted to those who ensured that Germany wasn't getting done (again).

Kahn became an icon at the turn of the millennium, the precise time when German football experienced its biggest post-war crisis of confidence. We were no longer good enough to score against the big boys then, but thanks to the crazed genius of 'King Kahn' the true extent of our vulnerability was not exposed. He was never a 'Keeper of Dreams', as Ronald Reng's brilliant book about Barnsley's German goalie Lars Leese would have it, but somebody who kept the nightmares at bay. Kahn saved us from the footballing equivalent of gang rape.

The (ever so slightly homoerotic) joys of 'coming from behind' could never catch on in Germany, where the idea of pleasurable pain lost all its appeal in the wake of the Holocaust. For a nation of perpetrators, it was both politically imprudent and psychologically impossible to adhere to the Protestant notion that suffering was virtuous.

Unencumbered by this ideological imperative, German football does not avert its gaze when it comes to the sexy side of things. Would Mario Gomez, the Stuttgart and Germany striker, have faced this much public scrutiny in England after his curious goal against Bayern Munich in 2007–08? When he was hit by a cross, the ball bounced off his groin area and into Oliver Kahn's net. Asked to locate the exact body part later on, Gomez was a little embarrassed. 'Somewhere between the thighs and the belly,' he volunteered gingerly. When pushed further, the slightly flustered striker admitted using his 'middle-thing'. 'It's big and it was hurting,' he smiled. That was much too subtle for *Bild*, of course, who enthused over the FIRST BUNDESLIGA GOAL SCORED WITH PENIS! the next day.

And whereas in Germany managers often lament that a certain *Torgeilheit* (Friedhelm Funkel at Eintracht Frankfurt) had been missing in their team's performance, the expression 'horny for goals' has yet to gain any currency in England. Here, the more agreeable 'lack of penetration' gets the blame for defeats, and the conceptual metaphor at the heart of that expression is rarely made as obvious as it was in a Hugh McIlvanney *Sunday Times* column. 'It was eunuch football,' he scoffed about England's futile goal attempts, 'without the slightest promise of meaningful penetration.'

Ian Holloway's verdict on Queens Park Rangers' rather dreary 3–0 victory against Chesterfield in August 2003 was equally instructive. 'To put it in gentleman's terms, if you've been out for a night and you're looking for a young lady and you pull one, you've done what you set out to do,' ventured the QPR manager. 'We didn't look our best but we've pulled . . . Our performance today would have been not the best-looking bird, but at least we got her in the taxi. She may not have been the best-looking lady we ended up taking home, but it was still very pleasant and very nice, so thanks very much and let's have coffee.' Holloway's unusual analysis, which in Germany might have been grounds for dismissal, caused much hilarity in England. Because that is exactly what happens every weekend throughout the country from Carlisle to Penzance: after a few beers you jump into a taxi with somebody – no matter who, best not to take that close a look. But people also laughed because his analysis, like most good jokes, played on a hidden truth. Bad football is like bad sex: without climaxes. The drabbest, most unwatchable 1–0 win will still leave a supporter satisfied in a way that the most riveting goalless draw never can.

Charlie George (Arsenal) rated the feeling of being cheered on by thousands of fans at Highbury as 'better than sex'. George was one of the most talented footballers of the early 1970s, a long-haired rebel who on a good day could play as elegantly as Beckenbauer and as extravagantly as Cruyff. As a boy he had stood on the terraces at Highbury; he was the textbook local hero. In the European Cup he scored four times against Real Madrid, and during extra-time in the 1971 Cup final against Liverpool he scored one of the most legendary goals in English football history. His shot sizzled into the net from twenty-five yards to decide the match for the Gunners. His celebration has become even more famous. The then twenty-year-old lay down on the pitch, his arms and legs outstretched, and waited, grinning, for his team-mates. In one of the photos it looks as if he had an erection. 'King' George says he was simply exhausted.

CHAPTER 2

Handbags at Dawn: The Tragedy of the Technicians

As we have seen, the Victorian hostility towards pleasure cannot on its own be held responsible for the cultural hegemony of warriors and tacklers. In truth, Reverend Thring's anti-individualistic ideology of purity, which condemned solitude as the first step towards masturbation, had almost no effect on the way the game was played at first. On the contrary, football in the public schools was dominated by dribblers. Players took the ball and tried to reach the opponents' goal on their own. Team-mates ran behind or beside, and continued the dribble if the first dribbler lost control of the leather. Dribbling was not seen as obstinate, but noble. In the 1870s, Eton's school newspaper criticised the 'unsporting' playing style of working-class teams who preferred to pass the ball. Players who gave the ball away absolved themselves of individual responsibility – that was seen as cowardly and unmanly.

In Lord Northcliff's *War Book* from 1917, the natural superiority of British troops was related back to football. '[The Germans'] whole training from childhood upwards has been to obey, and to obey in numbers,' he wrote. 'He has not played individual games. Football, which develops individuality, has only been introduced into Germany in comparatively recent times.'

In truth, however, the golden age of dribbling was already over by this stage. The working class had monopolised the sport, professionalised it, and changed the style of play for good. The old idealists were only left with the memory of better days. 'The professional game is based on mechanical activity and laborious training,' complained *The Annals of the Corinthians Football Club*. 'The amateur relies on his natural spirit. The amateur is independent. It is his independence and education at public school that distinguish his style of play.'

Work? Not for gentlemen. Training? Only for the masses, if you please. This undisguised snobbery was a reaction against the new mentality of the professional clubs. Industrialists and big businessmen took command. They loved the sport as much as their employees did, but had few altruistic motives. Through football the workers became fitter, and victories were good for work morale. The requirements changed. A player no longer had to show artistry, but a high 'work-rate'; he became a worker in shorts, the game a collective endeavour.

Productivity on the pitch – i.e. victories – soon became more important than anything else. The formations reflected this. Whereas in 1850 the prevailing system had been 1-9 – a single defender and nine dribblers – around the turn of the century teams were already playing a 2-3-5 system. The long-pass game, developed by the Scottish team Queen's Park and later adapted by Preston North End, made ever more defensive formations necessary. The less your opponents dribbled, the more men you needed to defend your own half. By 1925, Newcastle United's offside trap was so successful and functional 'collective football' had evolved to the point that the offside rule had to be relaxed: only two players instead of three now had to be between the attacker and the goal line.

Arsenal manager Herbert Chapman pulled back another midfielder into defence, and in the 1930s won five championships and two FA Cups with his comparatively defensive 3-2-5 system. This 'WM' formation – defenders and midfielders were arranged in a 'W', the five forwards in an 'M' – remained the standard pattern until Brazil's victory in the 1958 World Cup.

There was still room for individualists, but not much. Sir Stanley Matthews's style of play was the shining exception that proved the increasingly sober rule. 'The Wizard of the Dribble' was an exceptionally gifted right winger and the perfect gentleman. He played his first match when he was seventeen, his final one when he was fifty. In just over 700 games for Stoke City and Blackpool he did not receive a single booking. Matthews played in shoes made especially for him, which were much lighter than the normal boots of the time. His progressiveness fed on nostalgia: Matthews played the football of yesteryear and was an unreconstructed romantic in a sea of pragmatists. He would have been the perfect role model for all successive generations around the world. If only the Hungarians had not been so good.

On 25 November 1953 this great side, which included Nándor Hidegkuti and Ferenc Puskás, defeated the English 6–3 at Wembley. The Magyars played football as if they were from another planet, highly imaginative combination play that was technically miles superior to that of their hosts. The result shattered the English myth of invincibility on home turf that had been carefully constructed with a selective approach to history (in 1877 the Scots had already beaten England 3–1 in South London), and came as a severe culture shock. Six months later, Walter Winterbottom's side was humiliated 7–1 in Budapest. England had finally woken up from her dream. When the national side reached the quarter-finals at the next World Cup in Switzerland, it was considered a minor success.

National manager Winterbottom drew the right conclusions from the disaster. He implemented the policy whereby the manager and two other officials picked the national side rather than a committee of nine from the Football Association. He recommended more individual training, more modern facilities and more youth work. The FA lacked the political and financial means, however, to carry out this structural reform. The balance of power in football was with the clubs, and they had no interest in fostering the national team.

Although the fundamental tactical and technical deficits were not reduced in the years that followed, the climate changed sufficiently for technicians such as Len Shackleton, wantonly ignored for ages, to be invited back into the fold. He had been overlooked for five years because his style of play did not correspond with the ideas of the selection committee. Individualists were not wanted, an FA official had told him; they were looking for men who played the ball as quickly as possible. 'It was an unpardonable sin for players such as Stanley Matthews or myself to use our skills to beat opponents,' the 'Clown Prince of Football' recalled in his memoirs.

In December 1954, England defeated the seriously weakened German world champions 3–1. With Matthews, Shackleton and striker Tom Finney, they had three distinct individualists in the team. A 3–1 victory in Berlin in May 1956 sparked hopes for the World Cup in Sweden. In February 1958, however, four regular England players died in the Manchester United air disaster in Munich, and without Matthews and Shackleton, who was out of the game with an ankle injury, England did not progress beyond the group stage. Four years later in Chile they were knocked out in the quarter-final by the eventual champions, Brazil.

In both of those World Cups, England were out of their depth against the international competition. The opponents were not only tactically more flexible than the English, who stuck rigidly to their plans, but also had better technical training. 'Coaches think directness, speed and fight are the three greatest virtues,' Finney wrote, 'but they emphasise them at the expense of skill with the ball.' After the World Cup in Chile, Winterbottom resigned. With their appointment of a new manager the FA could have given a sign and finally heralded the dawn of the modern age. But they chose Alf Ramsey.

Ramsey, a moderately talented but extremely enthusiastic defender, had played his last game for England in the Wembley debacle against Hungary in 1953. He did not share the general admiration for the ball magicians, and in his opinion there was nothing one could learn from them, either. 'Four of their goals were scored from outside the box,' he said dismissively. 'We should never have lost.'

The former Spurs player preferred to take his cue from the victories (won under questionable circumstances) of the Wolverhampton Wanderers side against leading eastern European teams in November 1954. At Molineux, the short-pass specialists Spartak Moscow were one of the sides to be floored when they lost 4–0. '[Wolves] did what we secretly hoped,' the *Mirror* rejoiced. 'They hammered, hammered and hammered Spartak until they were broken.' Eleven Wolves in England jerseys – that was the recipe for success for many observers.

As manager of Ipswich Town, Ramsey had led his modest team to the First Division title in 1962 with defensive football, and he believed that this negative system would also work for England. 'His formula was to deny the good footballers in the opposition side the opportunity to play their game,' Eamon Dunphy wrote. His tactics were so fixed on opposition strengths that the talent in his own team was routinely overlooked. The solution to all problems appeared to be not more technique, but less.

When in doubt, Ramsey preferred to go with hard men such as Nobby Stiles and Jack Charlton. In his new 4-4-2 system, which was almost exclusively aimed at curbing attacks by the opposition – the newspapers called the side the 'wingless wonders' – there was no room for Jimmy Greaves in the 1966 Wembley final. The more prosaic Roger Hunt, who was known exclusively for his strength, played in place of the creative striker, whom Ramsey always mistrusted. This choice of personnel was sadly symptomatic.

'Greavsie' was technically the most accomplished and most successful English striker of the 1960s. In fifty-seven games for his country he scored forty-four goals, and he won the 1963 Cup Winners' Cup with Tottenham, the first time a British side had triumphed in Europe. An old photo of the World Cup final at Wembley shows the entire English bench leaping for joy after the final whistle. Only Jimmy Greaves alone is standing there, po-faced, in his suit. He could have been one of the greatest goal-scorers of all time, an English Gerd Müller. He never got over Ramsey's decision and later became an alcoholic.

In 1966, the English were crowned kings of the football world. The mink coat soon proved to be a shirt of Nessus, however; a historical misfortune. 'English football was the real loser,' David Downing writes in *The Best of Enemies: England v Germany*, a wonderful book about German–English football rivalry. The Wembley victory legitimised Ramsey's destruction tactics and selection policy, and strengthened the 'English insularity' and the old values of toughness, speed and willingness for self-sacrifice. England were world champions and did not have to be taught anything about ball control by others. Not by Hungary, nor by any other spineless group of fancy foreign players.

'The lesson learnt from [Ramsey's] success was that exceptional work-rate, team understanding and defensive impenetrability could overcome more skilful but less effective foreign sides,' writes the football sociologist Chas Critcher. Even today, Ramsey is deified for England's first and only tournament victory. Only a few people can see the incredibly high price the country had to pay for this success. 'If we are going to accept a humourless, cynical, negative opportunist as one of our sporting heroes, of what calibre will the villains have to be?' asks the historian Frank McLynn.

When the 'General' failed to qualify for the 1974 World Cup finals in Germany and was relieved of his office, his totally reactionary football ideology had already taken hold. Everywhere else people were trying to copy the Brazilians, the Dutch, even the Beckenbauers and Overaths; only in England did talented street players continue to be treated like 'lepers', Winner writes.

The rise and fall of George Best, the 'fifth Beatle', symbolises the sad failure of the free spirit in football. With his irresistible dribbling and wonderful goals, the Northern Irishman had helped Manchester United secure the first English European Cup victory in 1968. He was a hero of the Swinging Sixties and on the way to becoming one of the top four or five players of all time. Then he lost his career to alcohol and countless amorous adventures. 'Bestie's' downfall was probably a result of his delicate personality structure. But he was not a unique case. A whole generation of lesser-known long-haired geniuses, who given their potential could have been greats of world football, went under alongside him.

Arsenal's Charlie George was only picked once to play for his country, and was substituted after half an hour. Gambling debts and alcohol drove him into destitution. Chelsea's Peter Osgood had made the Blues into the most attractive team of the late 1960s, and had led them to a Cup Winners' Cup (1971) and an FA Cup (1970). For Ramsey, 105 goals in 286 games were not enough: 'Ossie' only got to wear the three lions on his shirt on four occasions. His team-mate Alan Hudson was an elegant playmaker, far too stylish for the dry national coach. Ramsey's successor, the no less conservative Don Revie, gave Hudson his first outing as an England player in 1975 against Germany. The twenty-three-year-old, who in the meantime had moved to Southampton, played the game of his life as England won 2–0 at Wembley. Günter Netzer, the German midfielder, thought him 'a fantastic player with the potential to become world class'. Hudson was rewarded with another match for England, and that was it.

Flair players such as Frank Worthington (Leicester City, eight caps) and Rodney Marsh (George Best's congenial co-striker at Fulham, nine caps), who combined a wealth of ideas on the pitch with an anti-authoritarian mindset and a hedonistic lifestyle, were thorns in the side of the backward-looking football establishment. The newspapers disparaged them as unreliable 'stormy petrels' – strange creatures that would fly elegantly but were guaranteed to plummet as soon as the wind picked up – and titillated their readers with the players' escapades in typical tabloid fashion.

'Their crime was their sensuality,' David Winner writes of these discriminated-against artists. But first and foremost they faced another, more concrete problem. As far as the public was concerned they were too flash, too glamorous, too flamboyant, too conscious of their own ability. They were too quick to display their effortlessness. They played the game too colourfully. Although aristocratic or middle-class eccentrics are traditionally accepted in England, the rules for working-class men are less tolerant. Even in success they must remain modest, conscientious and predictable. You do not flaunt what you have, you don't stand out too much. It is not just society that demands this, but their own class, too.

Hudson and co. broke this taboo and had to pay the price. 'Players like Charlie George know what to expect on the pitch,' John Sadler wrote in the *Sun* at the beginning of the 1970s. In other words, players who showed off their talent so openly had only themselves to blame. Instead of offering an arena for the beauty of their game, football in the stadiums enacted a bigoted morality play. As the self-appointed guardians of traditional values, the hard men made a sport of hunting down the 'stormy petrels' and clipping their wings. Around this time, the phrase 'punishing tackle' was coined to describe particularly ugly fouls. In other words, physical assault was legitimised as a necessary sanction against those who played the game differently. Whoever violated the social order of football because of an excessive penchant for aesthetics had to be given a painful reminder of the true priorities of the sport.

Every Saturday, this incredibly bigoted Cops and Robbers game was played out afresh. Supporters in the stadium secretly crossed their fingers for the lawbreakers in their own side, while hoping that their hard men would give the opposition mavericks a brutal lesson in conforming to the system. 'Charlie George, Superstar, he walks like a woman and he wears a bra' they sang on the terraces. Even George Best's own fans occasionally wanted to know where he had left his handbag. Anybody who fought the opposition with esprit and wit rather than hardness could not be a real man; he was, and still is, a 'big girl's blouse'. Or, recalling the teachings of Reverend Thring, a wanker.

This primitive attitude – and a far too generous interpretation of the playing rules – turned flair players into fair game. They underwent years of torture at the hands of defenders, undiscerning managers and the media until, their nerves shot, they eventually gave up, drank themselves silly, or retired injured. It was the classic case of a self-fulfilling prophecy; the cliché transformed itself into an iron law: technicians were not up to much, they were not reliable. Trust nobody who can pass the ball further than thirty yards.

Under Ramsey's and Revie's disastrous leadership, the England team went into a steep decline in the 1970s, even though the country had half a dozen players who were a match for the Dutch and Germans. For the 1974 and 1978 World Cups, the English had to stay at home. In the league, clubs such as Manchester City, Manchester United and Chelsea, who allowed themselves a little more creativity, could not maintain success in the long term. Then, a somewhat different avant-garde bunch took power. As far back as 1976 Liverpool started playing the collective, straightforward and ultra-successful positional football that would blight the 1980s.

Rival English clubs had nothing to counter the indestructible Red Machine. Liverpool dominated the First Division until the beginning of the 1990s. On the European stage, the organisational strength of the Scousers also won through against more talented sides. This synthesis of toughness, application and tactical discipline also brought Nottingham Forest and Aston Villa great success: from 1977 to 1984 English teams won the European Cup seven times out of eight. Never was English football as assured of itself as in this dark age of 1–0 finals. These matches were won by teams, not great individualists; and it was usually Scotsmen or Irishmen who were responsible for the few flashes of inspiration.

One only needs to consult the list of English football captains to see the role models the country chose for itself. Martin Peters (West Ham and Tottenham) was the last flair player to wear the armband, in 1974. This talented winger was substituted by the over-cautious Ramsey at half-time during the 1970 World Cup quarter-final against Germany, when England were leading 2–0; in the second half the Germans turned the game around and won 3–2. After Peters, the captaincy was given to goalkeepers, uncompromising defenders, midfield workers and strikers who fitted either the 'loyal warrior' or 'noble knight' traditions. Outstanding players such as Kevin Keegan, Bryan Robson, Stuart Pearce and Gary Lineker were heroes of conformity. What made them exceptional was their ability to fulfil the two roles permitted much better than their team-mates. Genuinely creative talents of the 1980s, such as Glenn Hoddle – who was mockingly called 'Glenda' because of his cultured style – and Chris Waddle, continued to be excluded. Both of them fled abroad where their skills were better appreciated.

Paul Gascoigne (Tottenham, 1988–92) almost succeeded in breaking this pattern. His quick play, full of dribbling, anticipated a better future; and when he sobbed uncontrollably into the cameras after England's defeat in the 1990 World Cup semi-final against Germany, the nation took him to their hearts. 'Gazza' became the symbol of a renaissance. Italia 90 and the end of the five-year ban on English clubs in Europe after the Heysel disaster made football socially acceptable again, and led to a reorientation of the sport. After Gascoigne's move to Lazio, English television broadcast live matches every Sunday from Serie A. Beauty and technique were soon no longer swear words. The new Premier

League, dressed up by the millions pumped into it by the pay television broadcaster Sky, heralded the triumph of market forces: football became a product of the entertainment industry. And for all products, it is obvious that sex sells. Things sell better if they are sexy.

In the booming 'cappuccino years' before and after Tony Blair's election as Prime Minister (1997), England discovered an appetite for pleasure. Along with food, architecture and fashion, football became more relevant and better. Good taste was no longer something to be suspicious of, but a social imperative.

Gascoigne was not able to profit much personally from this paradigm shift. He had squandered the best years of his career with a tendency to self-destruct typical of British geniuses. By contrast, imported foreigners, who were technically light-years ahead of the native warriors and knights, were able to satisfy the new hunger for aesthetics. Eric Cantona, Gianfranco Zola, Dennis Bergkamp and Jürgen Klinsmann had to face the traditional resentment, too, but their success ultimately gave the critics little to argue with. And they were helped by the commercialisation of the sport. The big clubs had no desire to see their expensive acquisitions hacked down by unreconstructed defenders, and lobbied the FA for a more judicious interpretation of the laws. The era of the punishing tackle was over.

Yet the nation had to wait until the twenty-first century before another Englishman known for his exceptional technique (at least as far as crosses and free kicks were concerned) rather than 'blood, sweat and tears' was given the captaincy. David Beckham's promotion by interim manager Peter Taylor on 15 November 2000 was a milestone in English footballing history. 'Becks' broke down the old prejudices further, but he could not eliminate them entirely. Long before his legs started to give way, people said he lacked the nerve (for penalties) and the necessary self-control (he was the first English player to collect two red cards). These criticisms were tendentious: they reeked of Ramsey's England. His quality was not in doubt, but his grit, his courage, his manliness. When Beckham relinquished the armband in the wake of the disappointing World Cup in Germany, John Terry, the humourless and guaranteed unfeminine enforcer in Chelsea's defence, took over.

'At present, English football is in its most schizophrenic stage,' John Sugden says. 'On the one hand it wants to be modern, attractive and technically sophisticated; on the other it's uneasy about the changes that have taken place over the last few years.' Worries over the loss of identity surfaced in the discussion about the leadership of England's manager Eriksson, which was said to be too businesslike and clinical; and in the criticism of Beckham, the 'negative' tactics of Mourinho and Benítez, and Wenger's open preference for foreign players. In February 2005, Arsenal became the first club to play a league game without an Englishman in the squad.

Mr Campbell, the old hacker, still lingers in the soul. A pundit would praise Thierry Henry's magic skills, then cite the large quantity of gloves worn on the pitch (only by foreigners, of course) as the main reason for defeat. And because England believes that matches are won not in the head but in the depths of the stomach, rarely can a game pass without mentioning a player's fashion accessory: in the eyes of the viewers, there are just too many handbags around. A montage in the *Sun* from the 2004 European Championship game against France (Zidane scored to give France a 2–1 victory) showed England's wall anxiously clutching handbags against their bodies. The inference was that they were women, squeamish and afraid.

The same indignant tone is adopted whenever there is a minor brawl on the pitch or in the players' tunnel. 'A case of handbags at dawn,' the commentator will say, slightly piqued. If there is to be a duel, then please let it be a proper one: to the death. No girly shoving. No, no, it was only handbags, one of the players will confirm afterwards. He then laughs quickly, a little ashamed of himself. A proper beating would have been more fun.

CHAPTER 3

We Shall Not Be Moved

What do those who kick the ball around in a street have in common with astro-turf tricksters and Copacabana beach dribblers, apart from decent technique and an aversion to tackling? The answer is that their highly specialised style is a product of the geographical conditions – none of them play on grass. In England, by contrast, people only play on grass. There are of course artificial grass pitches, where office teams play in the evenings, but these are smaller, for five-a-side matches. Real football is played on green or muddy brown pitches, every weekend, in wind and weather. Only when the rare danger exists that the sun might come out does the ball stop rolling. From May to August goalposts are taken down everywhere, then people play cricket. Europeans laugh when they find out that football is officially England's winter sport.

With their under-pitch heating and scrupulously manicured turf, the big clubs are scarcely affected by the weather nowadays. You have to go down to the non-league divisions, or to Hackney Marshes (a former swamp in north-east London with eighty-seven football pitches for amateur teams), to see how much the English game is, or was, influenced by the weather. By the beginning of November at the latest, many pitches are already so furrowed that in the centre circle and outside the box you stand ankle-deep in mud. The ball frequently sits in huge puddles. It is not only the famous British rain that is responsible for this, but more importantly the packed playing schedule. Almost all the amateur leagues, following the model of the Premier League, contest league and FA cups in addition to their championship. The average public pitch is ploughed up three to four times a day each weekend, until not a blade of grass is left. Yet they still kick off. There is scarcely a referee or groundsman who applies the strictest criteria when judging whether the conditions are unplayable.

There are pitches little longer than they are wide, and some which go sharply uphill. After all, there is nothing in the rules about a level playing field. In North London, not far from the Tottenham Hotspur training ground – where the public can play at weekends – there is a field on a hill which not only descends steeply but also falls away to one side. Quite often, the coin-toss before kick-off will decide victory and defeat.

If a few match days are nonetheless cancelled – because the pitches are completely iced over, or an English monsoon has washed away the goalposts – the timetable is instantly put under so much pressure that it is necessary to schedule so-called 'double headers' at the end of the season. In this instance, two teams play two matches against each other back to back, each one lasting an hour. Or until the first ambulance drives on to the pitch.

Given these playing conditions it is not entirely surprising that England has not become the natural home of super-technicians. After the introduction of league football in 1888, the old dribbling game of the amateurs could not survive on a wide scale, if only because of the external conditions. The pitches, battered by many additional matches, made this type of play completely impossible.

Today, Sunday league football provides a glimpse of the professional game's past. Anybody trying to play a one-two in midfield or run past an opponent gets stuck in the mud and is instantly knocked down. Keeping the ball on the ground is not really an option. Back-passes are suicidal, the ball does not get that far. All that is left is the big punt forward. 'Put it back in the mixer!' amateur coaches scream at their full-backs prior to a cross. Less talented defenders are ordered to play 'percentages', a euphemism for hoofing it blindly out of their own box. For their part, the attackers try to prevent this and tackle the full-backs. Here, defence really begins in attack. Building slowly from the back, on these pitches? Ball possession is not a strategic goal, but a hazard – the presage to an opposition goal.

The classic kick and rush, or Route 1, is the simplest, most effective way to deal with these conditions, and was the style that dominated the sport until the late 1980s, when the higher leagues gradually discovered better pitch-care methods. Strikers had to be tall, broad and strong, to handle the high balls; the central defenders had to be tall, broad and strong, to shove the forwards out of the way. Whereas on the continent it was number tens, *fantasisti* or sweepers who made the play, the few Englishmen with ball skills were not only symbolically pushed to the side. They had to become wingers because the area along the touchlines was best suited to technical play. For all other players, the most important qualities were vigour and raw power, not technique. Anybody without the right physique – and the unfailing will to fight – drowned in the mire.

'Mud was also a potent and trusted weapon against foreigners,' Winner writes. Prior to the eagerly awaited visit of

Honved Budapest in December 1954, Stan Cullis, the Wolverhampton Wanderers manager, had the pitch watered until Molineux became a brown mud bath. 'We thought he was crazy,' Ron Atkinson recalls. The future Manchester United coach was at the time a youth player at Wolves, and had been ordered to put a sprinkler on the turf. 'But when the match began I understood what his aim was. The Hungarians played the most wonderful direct football I had ever seen, and went into a 2–0 lead. But the pitch got more and more difficult. At some point they just couldn't get anywhere any more.' The English champions won 3–2. The heroic victory – they came from behind! – was, of course, judged to be a triumph of traditional English football. 'The genuine, original, unbeatable article . . . still the best of its kind in the world,' trumpeted the *Daily Express*. Real Madrid, Spartak Moscow and Dynamo Moscow were all defeated at Molineux in similar fashion. For Manchester United manager Matt Busby, the Wolves team at the time represented 'everything that was good in British football. They played with great power, with spirit and style. Their achievements against the best teams on the continent gave confidence to everybody connected with the game here. Stan Cullis created the team in his likeness. It was honest, straightforward, uncomplicated, full of lifeblood and determination.'

In these difficult, if not irregular, conditions the deeply rooted mistrust of individualists could only prove justified on football pitches week in, week out. George Best, technically the most accomplished Briton of all time, was fouled so often by the Scots in a game for Northern Ireland that he chucked a handful of mud at the referee in frustration, and was sent off. It was a silent cry for help and an eloquent complaint against the combination of brutality and mud that destroyed the game at the time.

Watching the DVD of the 1985 Cup Winners' Cup semi-final between Everton and Bayern Munich today, the viewer is overcome by sheer horror. For ninety minutes the central defender takes the ball from the keeper and boots it without ceremony in the general direction of the motionless hunk of a centre-forward hanging around the opposition box. The highly talented midfield at Goodison Park can only look on as the ball sails above their heads into the goalkeeper's arms every few seconds. For those watching, the horror is particularly manifest as it is unexpected: the team exhibiting this shocking anti-football was none other than Bayern. Everton, who came back from 1–0 down – a Dieter Hoeness fluke – and went on to win the cup, prevailed with hard but comparatively decent play on the wing – the ball was worked out wide as quickly as possible, and from there played back into the Bayern goal area. One or two combinations involving the full-backs moving forward were excellent.

This shocking example shows that in the bleak 1980s crimes against football were not only committed in England. And as long as pitch conditions allowed it, there were sides on this island that were not prepared to submit themselves to the *diktat* of Route 1. West Ham United, Tottenham, Chelsea and Manchester United all claimed – and still do – to be intrinsically good footballing sides, i.e. teams with an unusually friendly acquaintance with the ball. Brian Clough, who led Nottingham Forest to two sensational victories in the European Cup in 1979 and 1980, was also not a fan of the long ball: 'If God had wanted us to play football in the sky, he'd have put grass up there.'

In the late 1980s and early 1990s kick-and-rush football came into fashion again; it was a mercifully brief flourish. Vinnie Jones's Crazy Gang at Wimbledon were unsettling the First Division with coarse bombardments of the box, and even won the FA Cup. Charles Hughes, the author of the official FA coaching handbook, calculated back then that statistically most goals were scored from long balls. He preached 'PoMo' (position of maximum opportunity) – getting the ball as quickly as possible to the most dangerous area by the box.

In reality, however, this anti-style had already had its day. The pitches had become significantly better, Italia 90 had sparked the longing for a new, more artistic game, and with the advent of Sky and the expansion of merchandising the entertainment factor became ever more important. By the early 2000s the Premier League had emancipated itself from PoMo to such an extent that Gérard Houllier's Liverpool were mocked for the large number of long balls to striker Emile Heskey. ('Hoof!' the opposition fans jeered, which was not to be confused with 'Huuuth!', the war cry at Stamford Bridge in honour of German defender Robert Huth.) In the 2004–05 season, Bolton Wanderers were criticised for their many long throw-ins, and after Chelsea's 1–0 victory over Arsenal in August 2005, Arsène Wenger felt himself to be the moral victor, because the Blues' game, to his mind, had been 'too direct'. On several occasions José Mourinho's men had booted the ball to their lone attacker in classical, uncomplicated fashion. He then held on to the ball until the wingers Robben and Duff moved up the field.

At the very top, pure Route 1 is generally proscribed and discredited as a tactic. One level down – below the radar, if you will – English football has preserved its own unique ideology: it's still a very territorial game. At this level, in other words, territory is often more important than the ball.

What this actually means is not immediately apparent, but you can certainly hear it everywhere. The stadium crowd cheer every throw-in that is won deep into the opponents' half. Each corner is celebrated as if it were a last-minute winning goal. 'Box 'em in!' the coach screams when the opposition have a throw-in near their own goal. It goes without saying that before the game he will have impressed on his men the need to play in 'their half'. For the manager, a ball hit hopefully in the direction of the corner flag is 'a good ball' because it puts the opposition full-backs under pressure, and might result in a throw-in. Pushing back the opposition and gaining territory is not merely a means to an end but, as these reactions make clear, the actual, barely disguised objective. This overemphasis on the territorial aspect is a typical English anachronism within the modern game. The reasons for it can be found in the evolutionary history of football.

The first English football reports date from the twelfth century. Back then, whole villages assembled for matches, often after religious feast days. The ball was kicked or carried by the men, most of whom were considerably drunk, and all sorts of tackles were permitted, including stabbing opponents in the back. 'If that is what the English call playing, it would be impossible to imagine what they call fighting,' a French observer wrote. If the men had just returned from war, enemy heads from the battlefield were kicked through the streets. Many English pubs called the Saracen's Head evoke this unappetising custom. In Kingston-upon-Thames and Chester they preferred to kick round objects of Scandinavian origin – the severed heads of slayed Vikings.

The playing area could stretch over several miles. The goal was usually the gate of the neighbouring town, and the means by which the ball actually arrived there was irrelevant. This anarchic form of 'folk footballe', which a number of kings tried to outlaw in vain, was strictly speaking not a ball sport. The spherical object – usually a pig's bladder filled with feathers – was more of a movable banner, an instrument to measure the relative strength of the villages in this confusing battle. Its location determined success or capitulation in this mini civil war.

In the village of Ashbourne near Derby, an archaic form of folk football has survived to this day. Each year on Shrove Tuesday and Ash Wednesday the villagers living to the north of the river (The Up'ards) compete against the inhabitants of the other side (The Down'ards). The ball, handmade every year for the occasion, is rarely kicked, but moved around from place to place by the masses. Originally the goals were the water wheels of two mills. Today they are specially made steel constructions. The centre spot is in a supermarket car park.

Football-related games, such as the 'Eton Field Game', still exist in a few elite public schools. These appear to be a mixture between football and rugby, but are in fact the ancestors of the two modern sports.

While the world got to know and love soccer as a user-friendly export of the British Empire whose rules were already fixed, the sport in Britain could not – and did not want to – free itself completely from its muddy evolutionary history. The primacy of toughness in football's value system discussed in the first chapter is a direct consequence of this typically English, self-conscious preoccupation with the game's origin. A second, no less important consequence is the affinity – concealed for reasons of civility – with the fundamental idea of folk football: the conquest of opposition territory.

A frequent explanation given for the popularity of American football, rugby's North American cousin, is that the sport replays the original drama of the nation: the territorial acquisition of the pioneers and their trek westwards. With its two goals, football is a little more abstract in this respect, but the historic symbolism is still closely related. 'Serious sport . . . is war minus the shooting,' George Orwell wrote in 1945 when the Soviet football team made a tour of Britain. The author of

1984 criticised the chauvinism inside the grounds; for him international matches were 'a substitute for war'. For football in England more than anywhere else, this comment still has some validity. Here the game doesn't simulate a battle for territory, it *is* a game of war. Outside England this martial attitude will not be shared. Elsewhere football is a synonym for beauty, for *joie de vivre* and other nice things. Theoretically, the same could be true in Britain. But people do not want it to be like that.

Folk football and the pre-history of the sport can account for this mentality to a certain extent. But it can only be understood in its entirety if you include the country's history. In a nutshell: since the Norman invasion of 1066, England has not been conquered by a foreign power. For almost 1,000 years no critical military contest has been lost. The English could even deal with American independence, because they maintained economic control of the colony. The loss of the Empire after 1945 was not the direct result of a military defeat, but the indirect result of a victory: exhausted economically and militarily by the war, Great Britain no longer seriously opposed the nationalist movements in the colonies. The end of the Empire, undoubtedly a traumatic experience, crept up on the British as a political process. If there is one thing the English are afraid of today, it is a similar development, i.e. increasing European integration. But they are not afraid of war. Overall they have had too many agreeable experiences to really fear it.

After the catastrophic experiences of the twentieth century, Europeans do not like to talk of war. The English, used to victory, have a much more ambivalent, almost casual attitude towards it. *Plus jamais la guerre, Nie wieder Krieg* – there is no English equivalent to these pacifistic terms. On the contrary, the English are proud to describe themselves as a 'warrior race'. Which Western nation would want to assert itself in this way in the twenty-first century?

The warriors' newspaper of choice is the *Sun*. The bloodthirsty, ultra-chauvinistic headlines of this paper are legendary. GO GET 'EM, BOYS! it urged during the Gulf War; after the sinking of the Argentinian warship the *Belgrano*, the headline was, GOTCHA!; and then there was UP YOURS, DELORS, aimed at the president of the EU Commission. When the going gets tough, the paper quickly mobilises the foot-soldiers on the home front. The Ministry of Defence could not do a better job.

As a German who enjoyed a typically liberal upbringing, I can only look in astonishment at such deranged propaganda. In England people do not even consider it such. 'We're just supporting our troops!' It is seen as totally normal and legitimate. Like the hardcore fans in the stadiums, the *Sun* is just providing the slogans.

Military contests have a prominent place in the collective psyche because recollection of them is generally speaking not traumatic. On the contrary, it is a source of positive identity and comforting. In every city, streets and squares are named after the great victories of Trafalgar, Waterloo and Agincourt. Even the disaster of Dunkirk, when in 1940 over 300,000 British and Allied troops had to be evacuated, is immortalised on every major street plan. Those who win wars also find it easier to commemorate lost battles. In Liverpool (Anfield), Leeds (Elland Road), Sheffield (Hillsborough) and Coventry (Highfield Road) stands were named after a terrible defeat in the Boer War. In 1900 at Spionkop-Berg (now in South Africa) more than 300 British soldiers were killed, and more than 1,600 were wounded. When they returned home, survivors baptised the stands erected by their football clubs 'The Kop' in honour of their fallen comrades.

That all seems a little strange today, yet it fits perfectly with the favoured masculine ideal of the valiant warrior. Football simply had no choice. It had to associate itself with the battlefield, it had to be like war, if it wanted to establish a permanent and credible focus on the grit and courage of its players.

During the Christmas ceasefire of 1914 the famous football match between British and German soldiers took place. At the same time, however, the First World War highlighted far more explicitly the ideological kinship between sport and warfare. In 1915, troops from the 1st Battalion of the 18th London Regiment stationed in Belgium dribbled with footballs through no-man's land, past wounded comrades and towards German cannons. 'We kicked off and rushed the Turkish guns, dribbling the ball with us,' wrote one English soldier who fought at Gallipoli, the famous battle for the Dardanelles. On 1 July 1916, before the Somme offensive which would claim 1.2 million lives on both sides, Captain W. P. Nevill, commander of the 8th East Surreys, gave out four footballs to his men. On one of them was written 'The Great European Cup, The Finals, East Surreys v. Bavarians. Kick-off at Zero'; on another the inscription was 'No referee'. Nevill offered a prize for the first platoon to dribble into the German positions. When the machine-gun fire broke off, one soldier climbed out of the trench, booted the ball a long way forward and asked his comrades to run after it. 'A good kick,' one comrade wrote in admiration. 'The ball rose and travelled well towards the German line.'

'The long-ball game proved no more efficacious for the Surreys than it would for later English teams,' David Downing writes. 'Sixty thousand Englishmen fell on that first day of the Somme offensive, Captain Nevill and many of his Surreys among them.' Two balls were later found and put in a museum. An anonymous poet immortalised the audacity of the Surreys in appropriately dramatic lines:

> On through the hail of slaughter
> Where gallant comrades fall,
> Where blood is poured like water,
> They drive the trickling ball.
> The fear of death before them
> Is but an empty name.
> True to the land that bore them –
> The SURREYS play the game.

The central thesis of Downing's book *The Best of Enemies* is that, after their defeat in the 1966 final, the Germans, who basically played a similar style of game to the English, focused on their technique and tactics while the English stuck with their 'blood and soil' mentality and a manner of playing that went hand in hand with it. As a consequence, they remained trapped in footballing yesteryear.

'We have a deeply rooted anti-intellectual tradition,' John Williams says. 'Managers were not used to coaching players. They didn't practise with them. Either they could play or they couldn't.' This attitude persists today. Neither Alex Ferguson nor Martin O'Neill (Aston Villa) think it necessary to lead training sessions every day; they leave it to their assistants. During the week, many managers prefer to play golf or sit in their offices negotiating transfers. The lack of decent English goalkeepers is no coincidence: until a few years ago only a handful of clubs had specialist coaches. Foreign managers found it easy to take over.

Whereas in Germany every major defeat gives rise to knee-jerk complaints about the lack of top footballers, or doubts about the players' character, in England it is always a lack of fighting spirit that is held responsible for humiliating results. After the shameful 1–0 defeat in the World Cup qualifier against Northern Ireland in September 2005, Jeff Powell in the *Mail* heaped praise on the men in green for their warrior spirit and described Eriksson's men as pampered cowards: 'The multimillionaires who they challenged to battle were so befuddled by the constantly changing playing systems that they did not even manage to satisfy the minimal demand of every English team over the past centuries – they didn't have the bottle for battle.' The moral of the story: tactics is another word for weakness.

As is technique. 'I hate all that,' writes Dunphy about Millwall's effortless 5–1 victory against Preston North End in 1973. 'Every man [was] doing his party tricks. Indulging himself, flicking it here, flicking it there, beating a couple at a time, crossing it, having a shot. Taking it down on your thigh or on your chest.' Taking the ball on your chest? Disgusting. 'The one thing about English football is that you have forty-two battles, more or less. Battle is what the game is all about in the Second Division. And you come to have a taste for it, to enjoy it. And you tend to get turned off by something that is too easy.'

In defiance of much progress on the pitch, football terminology is still dominated by military metaphors. Pitches saturated by rain are routinely compared with the First World War battlefields of Passchendaele and the Somme. A *Daily Telegraph* reader who campaigned for Stuart 'Psycho' Pearce's inclusion in the best Premier League side of all time emphasised that the defender had the heart that 'you needed in the trenches'. A goalkeeper who squares up to a striker bearing down on him is 'standing his ground'. Like a battlefield, the football pitch is the 'place to stand up and be counted, there is nowhere to hide'. If little is happening in the goal mouth, it is a 'phoney war', recalling the idle phase in the Franco-German conflict prior to the invasion by the Wehrmacht in 1940. If the defence is steadfast, we hear of a 'rearguard action'. If in doubt, a defeat was not deserved, but 'brave'. Hopeless, inadequate resistance by the losers is generously credited as courage. And English teams do not come away from a match with a draw. The home team (or the clearly stronger, i.e. more attacking side) 'were held'. Like the Mexicans at Fort Alamo.

Do the multicultural teams of the Premier League actually understand the jargon? It is obvious that they at least feel what is going on in the stadiums. The English fans valiantly hold up their banners – the warrior ethos is celebrated, it lives on inside them practically undiluted. Before kick-off they scream as if possessed; not to voice support for their own team but to terrify the opposition like people do in old war films. (The wall of noise which hits away teams at Old Trafford or Anfield does not simply work on a psychological level. Human beings are two-thirds water that can be made to oscillate by massive sound waves. The sound of a large English stadium literally soughs through your heart and stomach. In China, there is a kung-fu fighter who can actually knock over opponents with a battle-cry uttered at a particular frequency. Infrasound, sound waves at a particularly low frequency that the human ear cannot detect, can destroy internal organs and are used by the military to make the enemy battle weary.)

Chelsea fans call themselves the 'Blue and White Army', Manchester United fans the 'Red Army', Newcastle United fans the 'Toon Army' ('Toon' is slang for town, the city of Newcastle). One of the most popular songs inside stadiums is to take the name of the manager followed by the club's colours and 'army'. Fulham fans, for example, sang 'Tigana's Black and White Army' during the UEFA Cup match against Hertha

BSC in December 2002. ('Why are they singing "Tigana, go away?" a Berlin reporter wondered in the press box.)

Moreover, fans in Britain rarely describe themselves merely as 'fans'. They are supporters – auxiliaries, if you will, who assist their elite unit on the pitch. Modish dreck such as good technique, the primacy of ball possession, or counter-attacking tactics has not changed the fact that 'in England, the cry is permanently to move forward', as Robert Huth says. 'Attack, attack!' they shout at Anfield; the bloc of away fans respond with 'We shall not, we shall not be moved', the old war-cry of the unions. We will not give in, we will not be put to flight.

As in any military campaign, troop numbers are decisive. Attending the game, particularly away from home or abroad, becomes a question of personal obligation. It is a call to muster. In fanzines, even peaceful troop members rave about the successful mobilisation of the previous week: 'We took 5,000 to a midweek game in Norwich! We took their ground!' 'Ground' refers to the stadium in England, but also to the land. Both can be conquered, and both have to be defended against intruders. Many fans really view the stands as their property, since they have either paid for them with donations or, as in Luton, built them with their own hands.

In 1981, the zoologist and former chairman of Oxford United Desmond Morris was certain. A Scottish fan who stormed on to the opposition half of the pitch brandishing a flag was 'nothing more than an unruly nuisance [to the authorities], but in his imagination he is no doubt a young warrior running bravely through enemy fire on some historic battlefield'.

John Williams does not believe that this fixation with territory can be explained using an anthropological approach. 'The men are not merely defending their territory instinctively, like animals. It is not about space as such, but what it represents. The club or the district is an integrative element of working-class pride; a culture that puts emphasis on pride in one's own roots and community.' This is particularly true of the post-industrial cities in the north of the country, the cradle of the modern game. The joint use of a stadium, objectively the most sensible and economic solution for local rivals, whether in Milan, Rome or Munich, is absolutely unthinkable in England. You do not move in with your enemies.

In his book *The Football Man*, the sociologist Arthur Hopcraft writes, 'By the 1920s football was an established employer in a community where jobs were scarce. The clubs had grown up out of pride in athleticism, in local importance, in corporate endeavour. The stadiums were planted where the supporters lived, in among the industrial mazes of factories and hunched workers' houses. The Saturday match became more than mere diversion from the daily grind, because there was often no work to be relieved. To go to the match was to escape from the dark of despondency into the light of combat. Here, by association with the home team, positive identity could be claimed by muscle and in goals.'

'It's about your local area, your home,' Williams says. And you do not let anybody into your home. In the 1960s and 1970s working-class youths would keep watch at Underground stops; anybody who did not look as if they belonged there was beaten up. Back then this was called 'station duty'. 'Men from Burnley can recognise men from Blackburn by their smell,' Williams continues, 'even though the towns are five minutes away from each other and there is no visible difference between the inhabitants. But you cannot allow rivals to make themselves at home on your patch. That's humiliating. They're drinking in our pubs! They're taking the piss! We have to show them who's in charge! Otherwise others will come here and do the same. Otherwise they'll say we're soft.'

For some of these 'local chauvinists', symbolic means and methods are not enough. It is but a short step from imaginary membership of an army to a real willingness to fight. In England, supporters do not turn up to watch the match; in their minds they would prefer being part of the armed forces. This behaviour is easier to understand if you take into consideration the socialisation of the natural football audience. '[Working-class kids] had no real concept of passive appreciation. They hadn't grown up being entertained by books or trips to the theatre, museum or gallery, they enjoyed events in which they were involved, where they were participating. Even football was not strictly a spectator sport for them; they stood on teeming ends as part of crews, their chanting and their singing, even their taunting and fighting, an integral part of the event,' Robert Elms writes in his book *The Way We Wore*.

Early studies on hooliganism highlighted the ritualistic components of fan fights and mostly ignored the real violence. According to the sociologists Peter Marsh, Elizabeth Rosser and Rom Harré, hooligans adhered to 'rules of disorder'. These stipulated that a conflict would run along regulated, symbolic lines, and would only get 'bloody' in case of an 'accident' or if the police intervened. This well-meaning interpretation was no longer valid by the middle of the 1980s when almost every game led to riots.

The objectives of the 'mimetic war games', as John Sugden calls them – chasing away the enemy, conquering the stadium – did not *per se* require violence, but could only very rarely be achieved by peaceful means. It became the norm, for example, to storm the away fans' section. Particularly hard 'crews' even dared to carry out kamikaze attacks on the home fans. This battle for the stands was known as 'taking their end'. It was nothing more than 'folk football' taken to its logical extreme: the violent conquest of territory, without a ball.

These cockfights led to one of football's greatest catastrophes. In May 1985 at the Heysel Stadium in Brussels thirty-eight Italian spectators and one Belgian died after Liverpool fans in the neighbouring Y section tore down a fence and stormed section Z, which was mainly full of Juventus fans. Under the pressure of fleeing spectators a wall collapsed. The victims were crushed or battered to death.

On the official Liverpool website it is argued that external conditions were responsible for that black day. In addition to the dilapidated state of the stadium, they criticise the fact that Italians were able to buy tickets for the neutral section Z. Heysel, the implication is, was a most regrettable accident. For a long time the mantra that 'the wall was to blame' was what Liverpool fans believed, too.

Tony Evans thought this to be the case for many years. Now *The Times* football editor, Evans had gone along to Heysel as a fellow Reds supporter. 'Many Scousers had made it into the stadium without tickets,' he wrote in April 2005, on the occasion of the Champions League quarter-final between Liverpool and Juventus. 'We looked enviously at the space in section Z . . . There were too many people in our section. I went to the toilet and, by the time I came back, the fence was down and people were climbing over. Unable to locate my group, I joined the swarm. In section Z I wandered around for a while. There seemed to be very little trouble. People backed away but there were no charges, just a minor scuffle or two.' Evans returned to his section without being aware that any serious violence was taking place. A little bit of aggro, nothing out of the ordinary. The Italians fled from section Z, the Liverpudlians stood victoriously in the stand, but Juve won the match 1–0. He only found out about the deaths the following day; and only several years later did it dawn on him that the taking-their-end game was to blame for the disaster rather than the rickety wall.

In the wake of Heysel, the authorities made the separation of fan groups their top priority. Fences became higher, ditches deeper. In England, fans were crowded together in cages. Ken Bates, the belligerent owner of Chelsea, even wanted to electrify the fences and dig water trenches. 'Taking their end' disappeared almost completely from the stadiums, but the lack of room to manoeuvre was just as serious a problem. The stands turned into death traps. Just a few days before Heysel fifty-six people died when a wooden stand burned to the ground at Bradford City's Valley Parade. The investigation that followed revealed that two emergency exits had been illegally locked. Four years later the greatest disaster in the history of English football occurred.

At Hillsborough in Sheffield, Liverpool and Nottingham Forest were due to play an FA Cup semi-final. Just before kick-off many of the Liverpool fans had not yet entered the ground. The police lost their nerve and opened a second gate, through which thousands of Scousers thronged into the Leppings Lane End. Hundreds of people were pressed against the fences and injured, and ninety-six died – on live television. Hillsborough marked the sad nadir of football's bloodiest decade. Margaret Thatcher's government set up a board of inquiry that recommended getting rid of the terraces. Italia 90 was the first major tournament that had no standing tickets. The fences were pulled down, the fans freed from the cages.

Harsher police sanctions and more rigorous video surveillance alone did not prevent 'taking their end' from returning to the stadiums. After Heysel and Hillsborough the fans understood just how dangerous it could be to play war games in the stands. There were still tussles away from the grounds, but these were far less frequent than in the 1980s and involved fewer participants.

It is not entirely a coincidence that the most serious problems now occur abroad, when neither the external control mechanisms (police) nor the internal ones (caution) function properly. 'Sociologists speak of an "outer-structure experience",' says John Sugden. 'In these situations people do not feel bound by the normal rules.' This escapism principle basically applies to all men when away from house and home – and to women, too. But among English football fans this freedom combines with ancient fantasies of conquest to make a highly volatile mixture.

'They feel part of an expeditionary corps, part of a military adventure,' Williams says. 'I will never forget the time when television showed scenes from the riots in Charleroi [2000 European Championships] between German and English fans. One young Englishman, he might have been twenty, said to a Belgian policeman, "If it hadn't been for us you'd all be speaking German today." Us! It didn't occur to him that personally he hadn't played the slightest part in the liberation of Europe.'

In his book *Among the Thugs* the American Bill Buford described how important the historical aspect is for English fans. During the World Cup in Italy he watched English supporters being beaten back by Sardinian police units. 'Then one of them shouted, "We're English. Why are we running away? Englishmen don't run" . . . A few supporters who had fled in panic then remembered that they were English – that was important. And they reminded others that they were English, too; that was important, too. Suddenly the crowd stopped, turned round and charged at the Italian police with a reinforced sense of their national identity.'

The animated series *Monkey Dust* on BBC3 brilliantly parodied this mentality. It showed English football fans watching historical documentaries about famous battles on a big screen in the pub, then enthusiastically bellowing out the names of the victorious generals: 'One Duke of Gloucester, there's only one Duke of Gloucester!'

Interestingly, even drunken hooligans stick to certain codes of conduct when it comes to fighting. This is in contrast to their German or Dutch counterparts. Relative to the number of brawls, deaths are very rare. Sugden says, 'Deep down the lads are not interested in physical harm but symbolic victories. They want to occupy space, demonstrate their strength, take the town. It only becomes fatal when different rules apply in other places and the English don't understand these properly. In Istanbul in April 2000, Leeds fans provoked the locals with the usual gestures and were stabbed in revenge.'

Five years later, almost exactly twenty years after Heysel, Liverpool fans were in firm control of Taksim Square in Istanbul. The atmosphere was relaxed and jovial. Copious amounts of alcohol were being consumed but there was not the slightest problem. The Reds had clearly not forgotten Brussels. But anybody looking a bit closer could not miss the fact that the Scousers had followed a tacit plan of deployment. They had climbed on roof-tops and held the strategically important points at crossings. As an advanced post, a small group had also taken over the top floor of a kebab restaurant, from where they had a view over the adjacent pedestrian zone.

Football in England will probably continue to be a game of war for some time. It is harder to tell whether football will still resemble the football people know here in the future. In the highly sophisticated Premier League the territorial element is being increasingly marginalised. The condition of the pitch is scarcely a factor any more as the playing areas are now so good. Arsène Wenger recently said he believed better training facilities have contributed to the deterioration in tackling technique. 'Before in training, it was muddy and wet, now it is always dry and you never see tackling in training.' Teams are also less hampered by the weather these days. Wenger built an indoor pitch at Colney to keep the wind out. In this way the players freeze less often and have more patience for tactical and technical exercises. Local rivals Chelsea erected a huge tent over an artificial grass pitch at their multi-million-pound centre in Cobham. In that nicely temperate 'dome' José Mourinho used to have them practise their runs and formations for hours on end.

Things are even progressing at grass-roots level. Simon Clifford, a sports teacher from Leeds, has established more than 600 'Brazilian Soccer Schools' (BSS) since 1997 in the UK alone, where children are taught the style of football played in Brazil: in small groups, always with a ball, and protected from the British weather inside a sports hall. 'Of course talent is important,' he says, 'but the reality is that the Brazilians are better simply because they do more training with the ball.' Clifford's dream is that one day the entire England national team will consist of BSS-educated players.

That might be the future. At present there is an ever-increasing divide between the professionals from all over the globe, with their excellent technical and tactical skills, and the heirs to the folk footballers, with their pitches that slope down to one side and are unplayable from November onwards.

CHAPTER 4

'Michael Must Have Picked That Up in Spain'

Highbury, February 1999. Arsenal against Sheffield United in the FA Cup. Thirteen minutes before the final whistle it is 1–1, all set for a replay at Bramall Lane. The Sheffield defender Lee Morris, fouled by Dennis Bergkamp, sinks to the ground with cramp in his leg. The physios come on to the pitch. Morris is soon on his feet again. Arsenal's Ray Parlour, known to his fans as the 'Romford Pelé', does what every professional footballer would do: he throws the ball back to the opposition. The spectators prepare to applaud – but what is this? Debutant Nwankwo Kanu from Nigeria, who has recently come on as a substitute, takes the ball, goes round a baffled defender and crosses wide to the Dutchman Marc Overmars who is completely unmarked. Overmars makes it 2–1 to the home team.

Scarcely a single fan celebrates. The two teams stare at each other in disbelief. When referee Peter Jones points to the centre spot, the visitors lose it. They surround the referee, shove him around, and there are scuffles with the Gunners. For a few minutes the match threatens to get out of control. The enraged Blades threaten to storm the pitch. After what seems like an eternity the match continues. Nothing of note happens. Arsenal are in the next round, Sheffield are out.

But Arsène Wenger does not want to win in this manner. Immediately after the game he offers a replay to his counterpart Steve Bruce. 'That was an accident,' Arsenal's manager says. 'Kanu did not know that Morris was injured.' Would it not have been easier just to let Sheffield score a goal, a journalist asks at the press conference? 'Two wrongs don't make a right,' Wenger says. He rejects the idea of replaying the match in Sheffield, however. 'We're fair. But we're not stupid.'

Ten days later Arsenal beat Sheffield for a second time. The score is 2–1 again, and again Overmars scores. Arsenal are into the next round, Sheffield are out. Wenger receives several fair-play awards for his gesture. Even FIFA, who do not look particularly kindly on such replays, are silent. Everybody agrees: never before in the history of English football has such a thing occurred, and it will never occur again.

Yet fourteen months later, 31,000 spectators at Goodison Park are witnesses to an even more incredible event. In the eighty-fourth minute West Ham equalise through Freddie Kanouté and are now in charge. Everton are barely holding on. Trevor Sinclair crosses to Paolo Di Canio who is completely on his own in the box. The Hammers' Italian striker shapes to volley it, but then breaks off his strike and catches the ball in his hands. He shakes his head and points at Paul Gerard who is lying on the ground outside his penalty area. A few seconds before Sinclair's pass the Toffees' goalkeeper had dropped to the ground with a knee injury. From the faces of some of the Hammers players you can see that they have no idea what is going on. On the touchline, Harry Redknapp rolls his eyes. The crowd rise to give a standing ovation. Gerard has to be substituted. The match ends 1–1. The entire stadium gives Di Canio a huge cheer as he leaves the pitch.

'I don't believe I've seen anything like it,' Redknapp says afterwards. 'He was bound to score. That was true sportsmanship. It's nice that that still exists. We could have used the three points, but I'm not going to strangle him.' Di Canio was overwhelmed with praise and accolades, but he did not fully understand all the excitement: 'It seemed like the right thing to do, but I didn't really think about it. A serious injury to any professional is far worse than losing two points.'

The fact that in Wenger and Di Canio two foreigners had shown such sportsmanship was the real sensation for many English people. Before, the consensus up and down the country had been that the invasion of Europeans in the nineties had not just brought better technique and a more professional work ethic to England but also those much-hated continental sins: diving, theatricality, cheating and endless rolling around the pitch after non-fouls. Conservative commentators such as Jeff Powell in the *Daily Mail* – who after Sven Göran Eriksson's appointment as England manager described Sweden as a 'nation of hammer throwers' – told their readers on an almost daily basis that foreigners rode roughshod over the noble spirit of sportsmanship, and that the Premier League was being reduced to the level of any other.

The Channel was no longer a natural barrier to this damaging influence. Football has this in common with disease: the nasty stuff always comes from abroad. Syphilis is the 'French disease', while rubella is 'German measles'. It is quite a surprise that the dive has not entered the lexicon as the 'German dive' in honour of Jürgen Klinsmann. Even a post-Marxist academic like Chas Critcher, who interpreted the 'escalating problem of indiscipline' in the 1960s as a direct consequence of the alienation of footballers from their working-class origins, was convinced that the European Cup made everything much worse: 'English teams in European competition found themselves up against tactics they had never met before, while their own more robust methods were penalised. Small wonder they responded in kind. So some of the worst elements of the continental game (more specifically the Latin game) were grafted onto the already diseased body of English football.' Time-wasting, walls not far enough back, sharp studs, complaining – all these, according to Critcher, were 'new patterns of behaviour' that led English professional football into 'a deep sense crisis by the late 60s'. A virus, introduced from Europe. Like foot-and-mouth disease.

All 'Latins' – Italians, Frenchmen, South Americans – are under fundamental suspicion of violating the rules of fair play. Because the accusation was for a long time a general one, it lacked bite until 1966. Then came the World Cup. And the quarter-final against Argentina at Wembley.

Already in the run-up to the game the press had portrayed the South Americans as unscrupulous villains. After the 0–0 draw with Germany, a match marked by a good deal of unnecessary hard play, the Argentinians had been booed mercilessly by the crowd. It was even worse during their 2–1 defeat of Switzerland. The Argentinians thought they were being unfairly treated and interpreted the English antipathy as a show of arrogance from the former colonists. Even the normal training session on the eve of the match had been cancelled using a flimsy excuse. The officials were too busy organising dog-racing at Wembley that evening, it was said.

The game itself was very rough, but not one-sided as far as fouls were concerned. Both sides fought with all the means at their disposal, above and below the belt. 'If you ever walked down a dark alley, late at night in a strange town, and felt yourself suddenly swing around to peer into a doorway not knowing quite why, you will know the feeling of being on that pitch,' Geoff Hurst wrote in his memoirs, a bit melo-dramatically. Afterwards, English players complained of having been pulled by the ears and spat upon; Nobby Stiles's brutal fouls and an embarrassing dive by Alan Ball were not mentioned.

In the thirty-fifth minute events escalated. Captain Antonio Rattin was sent off by the German referee Rudolf Kreitlein for insulting him. 'I want a translator,' is all Rattin is supposed to have said. The German ref later admitted that he did not understand a single word of Spanish. Argentina's captain refused to leave the pitch. It took eight minutes before the match could be resumed, because Rattin was talking to FIFA officials on the touchline. On the way back to the dressing room he wiped his hands on a British flag.

In the second half Argentina tried to keep possession of the ball. The 88,000 spectators saw the square passes in midfield as time-wasting and booed. There was no let-up on the fouls. Then Hurst scored the only goal of the game fourteen minutes before the end. The Argentinians were beaten and outraged. One player urinated in the players' tunnel, others wanted to storm the English dressing room, the rest of them trashed their own dressing room. The England manager forbade his players from exchanging jerseys with 'such people', and explained in a television interview that his team would not be able to display its best football until it came up against 'decent opposition' who also played football and did not behave 'like animals'.

The English press thought the result was the right one. The Argentinians had paid for their cynicism; the English had deserved their victory for their cool heads and stiff upper lips. An article in *The Times* under the headline DESTRUCTIVE ATTITUDE OF SOUTH AMERICANS castigated the visitors' flaunting of the rules and defensive orientation, but failed to remark on Ramsey's cautious 4-4-2 tactics or the fact that the brilliant Brazilians had been completely kicked out of the tournament by brutal European teams.

After analysing a video recording of this match, David Downing, author of *England v Argentina: World Cups and Other Small Wars*, concluded that the home team had committed thirty-three fouls, the Argentinians only nineteen. But the facts do not change the roles given to the two teams in all subsequent duels: the 'Argies' became the ultimate perfidious villains in, thank God, sharp contrast to the morally upright, noble English. For the creation of this particular footballing myth, the rivalry with the Gauchos was much more important than the English conflict with the Germans, who had comparatively speaking a better reputation.

In the years that followed the South Americans did their best to live up to the prejudice. The Intercontinental Cup finals of 1967 and 1968 – Racing Club Buenos Aires against Celtic, and Estudiantes Buenos Aires against Manchester United – were punch-ups disguised as football, in which even neutral observers thought that the Argentinians were the chief culprits. 'Ball possession here puts your life in danger,' said United coach Matt Busby after the first leg at La Bombonera, the cauldron of Argentina. The teams from Buenos Aires won the cup twice in succession but gained few admirers.

Two friendly games in the seventies deepened the animosity. In 1974 the match at Wembley finished in a 2–2 draw. The notorious Jeff Powell thought it a moral victory for the 'aggression, effort, competitive bite' shown by the English. In fact there had been a lot of fighting again. Captain Emlyn Hughes had provoked Ruben Glaria and received a black eye in return. In spite of a peace summit in the referee's dressing room at half-time, tempers were not calmed. At the end of the match somebody threw a tin at the referee's head, Hughes refused to swap his jersey, and the visitors left the ground to loud cries of 'Animals, animals!' Three years later La Bombonera welcomed the Englishmen by shouting 'Animals, animals!' The Argentinian newspapers described them as 'pirates', in reference to the mounting dispute over the Falkland Islands. After a punch from Daniel Bertoni, defender Trevor Cherry lost two teeth. Inexplicably, the referee showed them both the red card. The match ended 1–1. Both sides were confirmed in their views. Argentina's manager, César Luis Menotti, thought the English were a very poor side, defensive and technically incompetent. Back in Britain, the *Express* wrote that 'the Argentine puma has yet to be tamed'.

England was not permitted to play the role of the tamer as she did not qualify for the 1978 World Cup finals. But after the sensational move by world champions Osvaldo Ardiles and Ricardo Villa to Tottenham Hotspur – at the time there were Scottish, Irish and Welsh players in the First Division but no real foreigners, and certainly no South Americans – relations finally improved. The two Argentinians convinced all the sceptics and transformed Spurs into a top-flight team. When Argentina visited Wembley again in 1980 for another friendly game, things had relaxed so much that, just for a change, no punches flew and the English fans generously cheered the tricks of the nineteen-year-old prodigy Diego Maradona. A 3–1 victory for the home side did no damage to the good atmosphere, either. England were fêted in the press as conquerors of the world champions, and were singled out as favourites for the European Championship in Italy.

By the end of 1986 the whole world lay at Maradona's feet. The whole world? No! One island in the North Sea inhabited by obdurate eccentrics held out fiercely against the glorification of the false prophet. For the English, Maradona was not the best player of all time, he was a cheat. A fraudster of the very worst kind. Quite simply, an Argentinian. Ignominy personified.

According to Maradona, the 'hand of God' was at play when he scored his first goal in the quarter-final of the 1986 World Cup. By that he meant that, in his eyes, England's defeat was just desserts for the Falklands War. The *Sun*, however, proclaimed that 'a little cheat' had knocked England out of the tournament; Bobby Robson's side bore no responsibility for their elimination.

The statements made by those directly involved were a little more sophisticated. Gary Lineker admitted that he would have done exactly the same. Robson said, 'I'm sure we wouldn't have complained if an English player had scored that way.' Less was said about Maradona's second goal, an irresistible solo effort from the halfway line. Terry Butcher, on the other hand, thought that England's fairness was responsible for their exit. 'Perhaps we ought to have been more cynical and simply fouled him,' he said, implying that the Argentinians would have certainly done the same. The fact that for ninety minutes England had hacked down Maradona at every opportunity, and that referee Ali Bennaceur had overlooked a blatant elbow in Maradona's face by Terry Fenwick as well as the hand of God, was conveniently forgotten.

'Thugs [with] despicable bad manners . . . they are a disgrace to their country and the scum of the earth,' ranted the *Sun* five years later. Their colleagues at the *Mirror* even called for an international ban for the South American team. During a mini-tournament in 1991 at Wembley the by now traditional altercations had resurfaced. The English had begun with unnecessary fouls, and the technically far superior Argentinians had responded with concerted spitting – for English people the most unsporting behaviour imaginable, far worse than physical violence. Even today the nation gets far more worked up over a spot of saliva in the face than the most vicious bone-crushing tackle from behind, given the benefit of the doubt as a genuine attempt to win the ball. The game ended 2–2, but the result was irrelevant. 'When you play against such teams you have to expect that,' Gary Lineker said of the Argentinians. 'It's in their nature, there's nothing you can do about it.' The good old bogeyman was back.

The ineffable 'hand of God' was soon tapping England on the shoulder again. At least the *Daily Telegraph* was minded to recall it when, during extra-time in the France 98 quarter-final, José Chamot played the ball with his hand in his own penalty area, but out of sight of the officials. Not long afterwards England lost their nerve in the penalty shoot-out. 'Never outplayed, never outfought, never outsung, England are nevertheless out of the World Cup,' lamented Henry Winter.

Overall the match was pretty fair, but not without its controversial moments. Early on Diego Simeone accepted David Seaman's invitation to fall over his widespread arms and came out with a penalty. A little later Michael Owen fell to the ground in Argentina's penalty area, and Shearer converted the spot-kick to make it 1–1. Soon after the restart Beckham, on the ground, heeled Simeone half-heartedly in the thigh because he felt he had been provoked. 'The Argentinian collapsed on the ground as if he'd been hit by the 03.40 plane from Buenos Aires,' Winter huffed. Beckham was sent off. England stoically defended the 2–2 scoreline, and not without skill. Shortly before the end of normal time, a Sol Campbell header was disallowed – Shearer's elbow had strayed into the face of goalkeeper Carlos Roa. 'Clearly a goal,' said an astonished Terry Venables in the studio.

Then came the penalties. As in 1990 in Italy, and at the 1996

European Championship, England were eliminated, only this time it was not the Germans but the Argentinians who were better from the spot.

The real reasons for this heroic failure were soon found. 'With Beckham on the pitch we would have won,' manager Glenn Hoddle claimed. In his opinion, referee Kim Milton Nielsen had overreacted. The Dane had fallen for Simeone's clever charade. While the nation's anger was focused squarely on Beckham – people burned and strung up Beckham dolls – fans and the media went head over heels in their admiration for Michael Owen. His goal to make it 2–1, a slalom manoeuvre at deadly pace through the Argentinian defence, was perhaps the most spectacular goal ever scored by an Englishman at a World Cup. Only Latins scored goals like that. Amid the general rejoicing one important detail was overlooked: just like a Latin, Owen had won England's penalty with a perfectly executed dive. Roberto Ayala had not touched him. This is crucial, because without this dive it is very unlikely he would have scored the second, fantastic goal. In the slow-motion replay you can see how the Argentinians pull out of the tackle and almost give him a free passage, for fear that he might collapse to the ground again. Owen was written up as a superstar and later voted BBC Sports Personality of the Year. A true English sportsman.

It did not seem to occur to anybody that the usual casting of roles was no longer valid. Beckham had not managed to keep a stiff upper lip, and had lost his nerve like a Latin; Owen had clearly cheated. Yet the English media only chided the Argentinians for their poor sportsmanship. There was indignation over the fact that they had sung loud songs on the team bus and waved patronisingly at the English players.

The old order – the fair Englishmen on one side, the unfair Argentinians on the other – had always been a soothing ointment for national self-esteem, a mini-version of the battle between St George, the patron saint of England, and the dragon. Anybody who relies continuously on painkillers, however, runs the risk of becoming addicted to them. In 1998, nobody wanted to admit that an English international player had fallen to the ground in front of the world's eyes without any interference by an opponent.

Before the group game against Argentina in Japan 2002 everything was as before. HOW FOUL CAN THEY GET? the *Mirror* asked, and invited its readers to bet on when the Argies would start with their dirty tricks. Amusingly, the penalty Beckham scored to make it 1–0 was won again by the smart Owen, who had willingly tripped over Mauricio Pochettino's leg. Because the Argentinians did not protest, nobody bothered to take a closer look. Put them in different shirts, though, and they would have said 'he went over a bit quickly'.

It is the tabloids in particular – and we have to include television in this respect – who have lovingly preserved these double standards. After every dive made by a foreigner in the Premier League the clichés are rolled out like old carpets; if Rooney, Gerrard or Lampard go down, on the other hand, things are quickly glossed over. When, during an England friendly against the USA in summer 2005, Michael Owen, then at Real Madrid, fell over very unconvincingly in the penalty area, the BBC commentator John 'Motty' Motson immediately knew what had happened. 'Michael must have picked that up in Spain,' he said.

The size of a white lie shows its necessity. The unfair foreigners and the threat from abroad are utilised to mask a much more uncomfortable truth: the history of English football tells of a dramatic fall from grace. The rules were broken from the outset.

As we have already seen, the sport in its modern form was

invented in public schools in the south of England. In 1862 Eton old boy Charles Thring, brother of Reverend Edward Thring, published the first compact rule book with only ten rules. Rule one of *The Simplest Game* stipulated that players could not throw the ball into the goal with their hands. Rule two, on the other hand, allowed the ball to be stopped with the hand. Kicks were only to be aimed at the ball (rule three); no tripping or heel kicking was allowed (rule five). But how were such transgressions to be penalised? *The Simplest Game* makes no mention of free kicks, penalties or yellow cards.

Back then these things were unnecessary, explains N. L. Jackson in *Association Football* from 1899. In the golden age of Thring and co., 'in the very early days of the game, when it was chiefly played in the old public schools for boys, the rules were strictly obeyed, every offence was unintentional. The reason for this was no doubt the honourable behaviour cultivated by boys in the schools of the better classes. They were forbidden from gaining an unfair advantage over their opponent.'

This chivalry soon came to an end, however. After the establishment of the FA Cup (back then called the 'Challenge Cup') in 1871 and football's triumphal sweep through the industrial Midlands and the north, local pride and the will to win came to the fore. Although only amateurs were allowed to play, the best players were soon given underhand payments – it was the era of shamateurism. The expansion of the rules after professional football was legalised in 1885 is also a strong indication that 'playing the game' was no longer the most important thing. The new rules were necessary because nothing else could contain the soaring levels of unfair behaviour.

The introduction of injury-time is a good example. It's September 1891, and Stoke City are playing at home against Aston Villa. Seconds before the end the visitors are leading

1–0. Then a Stoke striker is fouled in the box – penalty! Villa's goalkeeper is quick to pick up the ball. He kicks it over the roof of the stadium and leans back casually against the goalpost. It takes the Stoke players a minute to realise what is going on. They scramble, but do not manage to retrieve the ball in time. The referee blows his whistle; Villa have won.

It was only after this outrageous event that the laws required penalties to be taken after normal time as well. The Corinthians, however, had no use for this rule change. This is because the amateur side made up exclusively of ex-public schoolboys from the south of England refused to take penalties at all – too simple, too unfair. They never played in any tournaments and never argued with the referee. If an opposition player left the field injured, or was sent off, a Corinthian immediately went off to make the numbers equal again. Until the First World War these gentlemen from the upper class were one of the best teams in the country. They provided many international players, and in 1903 they beat FA Cup winners Bury 10–3. Although the Corinthians were ultimately fighting a losing battle for noble values, they perfectly illustrated the fact that there were now two opposing camps in English football.

The south (London was the seat of the Football Association) stood for the noble ideas of the upper class and saw itself as a moral authority; the north of the country (seat of the Football League) was a hot-house for professionalism and the working class's passionate will to win. The tensions between these two strands still exist, but are more surreptitious. The clubs, for example, like to deride FA officials as the 'blazer brigade', an old gentlemen's club which is well meaning but no longer up to dealing with the demands placed on the rules today. On the other hand, football terminology betrays the fact that the custodians of the laws in

London have not given up the dream of a return to the old ideals. Only in England is an illegal but crucial tackle called a 'professional foul'. The adjective 'professional', which in everyday life has only a positive resonance, here becomes a by-word for bad, calculating, cynical. The implied snobbery is really quite astonishing and perhaps a little too obvious for a people as dedicated to politeness and diplomacy as the English. Political expediency and the need to keep the social peace demanded that open discussion of these tensions was circumvented. In foreigners, an outside group was readily available to shoulder the blame for the moral decline after the war.

In an essay following Arsenal's replay against Sheffield in 1999, football chronicler Hunter Daves wrote, 'The tradition in England is the same as everywhere else – you cheat as much as you can. When the ball goes out you raise your hand, even though you know that you touched it last. Players go down, especially in the penalty area, to con the ref. They push, pull, shove, kick, spit, insult. The only crime is to be caught. English players are not better than others; they're merely less cunning and subtle. And yet the myth still exists that English players practise fair play. Only because we gave the world that expression.' To be fair, this is a bit too harsh. There certainly is a degree of hubris and self-deception involved but it would be foolish to underestimate the very genuine moral obligation that the term 'fairness' represents.

Under manager Don Revie, Leeds United were a rock-hard outfit in the late sixties and early seventies. Their ultra-physical game should have made them the heroes of English football, but people still talk of them as one might of a delinquent family member. 'Leeds were too brutal,' says football academic John Williams. 'With their underhand tactics they crossed the barrier of what was acceptable. They kicked you when the ball was nowhere near, and tried to injure you deliberately.' Leeds's methods were successful, but their contravention of the norms was simply too blatant. Football England penalised them with cold repugnance. They remain, as Rob Bagchi and Paul Rogerson put it in the title of their sympathetic book, 'The Unforgiven'.

There is no question that England has a distinct sense of rules and justice, as well as humour. Not all Englishmen are funny, but all would (secretly) like to be. The same is true of fairness. There is something akin to collective pressure towards fair play. This is apparent in public debate, for example: politicians, sportsmen, artists, but also a random plumber interviewed in the street, instinctively begin their comments with, 'Well, to be fair . . .' That is as much part of daily life as the myriad of 'thank yous' when buying a newspaper. When players are brawling on the pitch or the referee is being molested verbally, the media ask why football cannot be played in the fair spirit of rugby, the favourite sport of the upper class. In rugby, decisions are accepted without dissent or reaction by the players. This comparison is only rarely made pejoratively; it expresses a burning desire.

In his book *The English: A Portrait of a People*, television presenter Jeremy Paxman tries to explain where this proverbial fairness comes from. His starting point is the aforementioned battle between St George and the dragon. An Englishman sees himself quite seriously and instinctively on the side of Good. According to Paxman, there is also the deeply rooted feeling of 'I know my rights!', because in Britain people have fought for personal liberties for centuries.

The arch-fear of an Englishman: somebody taking *his* rightful place in a queue. The actual personal disadvantage is not the issue here, but the violation of a most sacred social code. For the English love rules. In that, they are dangerously close in mentality to those 'order-obsessed' Germans, and therefore prefer to keep it rather quiet.

The rules governing football could *only* have been invented in England, the place where they tend to codify everything, from human rights to cricket. The paramount importance of regulations also explains why the nation did not get worked up too much about the pathetic penalty attempts by Beckham and Darius Vassell when England crashed out of the 2004 European Championship against Portugal, their latest *bête noire*. Public anger was instead directed at referee Urs Meier.

In the ninetieth minute the Swiss official rightly disallowed Sol Campbell's goal, as John Terry had clearly obstructed goalkeeper Ricardo. Everybody in the stadium who wanted to see it did see it; there was no discussion among the international media who witnessed the scene in the Estadio da Luz, the replay from the behind-goal camera left no room for doubt. Yet England felt they had been robbed (again). Meier, called a 'Swiss banker' by a *Sun* back page in Cockney rhyming slang mode, had to go into hiding for a few days because the tabloid set a whole army of hooligans on his back. Months later, *Times* columnist Gabby Logan was still claiming in a TV advertisement for the paper that England would have beaten Portugal 'if video evidence had been allowed'. As far as the English were concerned, Meier had applied the rules wrongly – in other words, he had disregarded them. According to the English version of events, Terry's challenge was completely legitimate. Hardly anybody in England seems to know that a goalkeeper is supposed to enjoy special dispensation in the six-yard box. 'It surprises me that people here don't know the rules,' Jens Lehmann said about the lack of protection for goalkeepers in the Premier League.

'The goalkeeper may not be jostled in the goal area,' it says in the German football association rulebook under law twelve,

'Illegal play and unsporting conduct' (p. 94, *DFB Fussballregeln 2008–2009*). Yet this is only a 'directive' of the German football association, a clarification of the rule governing obstruction. Liverpool manager Rafael Benítez, too, thought that 'there is a [FIFA] rule that says the six-yard box is for the keeper. He has priority.' The Spaniard was speaking in the aftermath of Liverpool's 2–0 win over Bolton in November 2008, but the papers did not pause to look into the claim. BIZARRE KEEPER CLAIM: BENÍTEZ APPEARS TO HAVE INVENTED HIS OWN RULES screamed the *Daily Mail*.

In truth, special protection for the goalkeeper is indeed missing in the English rulebook, there are no directives to that effect (see Chapter One for a possible explanation). For English people, therefore, Meier's European interpretation was incomprehensible. As the custodian of the rules he had failed them catastrophically. And what do you call people who disregard laws or rules? Criminals. Thieves. Cue a million WE WUZ ROBBED! headlines in the tabloids.

In the costume drama *El Cid* a dead Spanish knight (played by Charlton Heston) is strapped to his horse for the decisive battle. When the Berbers see the legendary warrior riding towards them, they take flight in terror. A myth that is actually no longer in good health can still exude enormous symbolic power. This is certainly true of fair play.

The first thing a German footballer admires about the Premier League is the (relative) level of fairness on the pitch. 'Nobody stays on the ground, nobody howls, nobody writhes about the place,' Robert Huth says. 'Although referees are far more generous with the whistle, there aren't really any more fouls,' Thomas Hitzlsperger acknowledged, 'because fair play works a corrective in your mind.' Because English football is assumed to be played 'with an open visor', as German football commentators love to say, that is indeed how the game is played. The ideal becomes an internal imperative and thus reproduces itself. Consequently it is no surprise that Wenger and Di Canio – foreigners, of all people – became the most shining examples of good sportsmanship over the last few years. Immigrants have a natural interest in adopting the cultural practices and norms of a country. Some become more English than the English themselves in the process.

Maybe English football really does have a similarly positive effect on the rest of the world. The Premier League is the television superpower, and fairness is an important part of its image. It cannot be proved empirically, but you do get the sense that there has been just a touch less rolling around and feigning injury in the Bundesliga ever since coaches such as Klinsmann or Felix Magath and English 'legionaries' and ex-legionaries started extolling the proverbial English fair play in countless interviews. God knows football can do with a modicum of idealism.

Perhaps there is no need to take it quite so far as Brian Savill, however. In 2001 the amateur referee was troubled by the one-sidedness of a Great Bromley Cup match in Essex between Wimpole 2000 and Earls Colne Reserves. Earls Colne were leading 18–1 when following a Wimpole corner, Savill himself ran into the box and hit a lush volley into the net to narrow the gap to 18–2. It was not enough to get Wimpole back into it, and the game ended 20–2. Savill later explained to the Football Association that he had just wanted to make the game a bit fairer, even things up a little, but they were not amused. He was suspended for seven weeks, and resigned in protest.

CHAPTER 5

Tea With Mr Football

Hammersmith, Fulham and Putney are villages that were devoured by London. If you want to get from north to south you have to negotiate the narrow high streets – no longer suited to modern traffic – that all look identical with their Gap outlets, Boots stores and Starbucks cafés; cloned, permanently congested non-streets. A few miles beyond Putney bridge, London, the eight-million-people monster, loosens its grip at last. There is a bit of green, a bit of generosity. You pass beautiful houses with sharp stones by the kerb, designed to stop people from parking on the grass. Here is the All England Tennis Club. Here is Wimbledon.

'I'm here to see Jimmy Hill.' That suffices; the barrier goes up.

Fifty yards away, between courts fourteen and fifteen, Jimmy Hill is heading for the dressing rooms, a racket under his arm. The septuagenarian's gait bears the hallmarks of moderately severe hip arthritis.

'Oh, you made it all right, did you? Marvellous,' he says.

In the members' lounge, oil paintings of former club presidents hang in gold frames on green wallpaper. A lady serves tea and coffee, accompanied by a few biscuits.

Marvellous. Jimmy Hill has the inflection and turn of phrase of a British bomber pilot in 1960s war films. He is a gentleman of the old school, somebody who would not hesitate for an instant to lay down his beige Marks and Spencer jacket in order to help a lady over a puddle. Even if that meant running the risk of not being able to get up again because his hip had fallen to pieces.

He is not called 'The Chin' without reason. All that remains of his little Lenin beard that only used to accentuate the extraordinary length of his chin is a grey moustache, but this powerful, far too long, far too large lower jaw . . . A miracle of nature. Hill would not be an Englishman if he had not come to terms with getting ridiculed as a walking streetlamp many years ago. In his autobiography there is a photograph of him riding. 'Spot the horse!' it says underneath. Self-deprecation is very important in Britain.

In his spare time, Jimmy Hill plays tennis on the famous lawns at Wimbledon, as befits a true member of the British establishment. Every successful revolutionary ends up here eventually, either as a knight, a peer or, like Hill, with an OBE conferred by Her Majesty.

A few decades ago 'The Chin' was the dominant personality in football coverage on television. Hill was presenter of *Match of the Day, the* English football programme. Later he became an expert summariser for the BBC at major tournaments. His last main appearance was in 1998 at the World Cup in France. A true patriot, Hill wore a Union Jack tie for the occasion. Next to Gary Lineker and Alan Hansen he unfortunately came across like an old man who no longer quite understood the ways of the world. Many people still remember his earnest assertion that the Romanian team had an advantage because all the players had dyed their hair blond: 'They can pick out their team-mates more easily at a glance.' Lineker and Hansen had difficulty suppressing their laughter. Following the World Cup, Hill's contract was not extended. Twenty-five years at the BBC were at an end. Hill has never understood why. 'What I said about the Romanians' hair made some critics and viewers doubt my sanity,' he writes with a hint of bitterness in his autobiography. 'But I think that this reaction showed a basic ignorance of our national sport.' Well.

Until a few years ago he was still able to proclaim his increasingly eccentric opinions every Sunday on Sky. *Jimmy Hill's Sunday Supplement* – 'Jimmy Hill's' was axed from the title, along with Jimmy, in 2007 – used to be a football chat show in a mock farmhouse setting; for undiscernible reasons, Jimmy half-heartedly pretended to be broadcasting from his house in Surrey. Brian 'Wooly' Woolnough, the gruff football editor of the *Daily Star*, led the discussion and was doing so even when Hill had top billing. Jimmy would get a little too caught up in his own thoughts to provide the programme with the necessary pace. His analyses were always just off the mark; the explanatory models from the past were no longer apposite. 'One doesn't really know whether Jimmy Hill is an institution, or if he should be put in one,' pondered Martin Kelner, the *Guardian*'s television critic. Like many former sportsmen or showbiz stars, 'The Chin' unfortunately missed the right point at which to chuck it all in. 'I just love the game too much,' he says with his enthusiastic, breezy Jimmy Hill chuckle. It is a chuckle that can be heard after almost every sentence, often for no apparent reason. He is somewhat strange, but very pleasant company. British people cannot stand arrogance but they always have a place in their heart for sad, fallen heroes. That explains why Hill was allowed to keep on broadcasting, to the point when watching him was not fun any more, but painful.

Not even his highly dubious defence of Ron Atkinson could

cost him his programme. Atkinson, a former player and manager, was in the expert's chair live on ITV for the 2004 Champions League semi-final between Monaco and Chelsea. After some chaotic substitutions and tactical suicide by coach Claudio Ranieri, Chelsea lost 3–1. After the final whistle Atkinson branded Chelsea's Marcel Desailly a 'lazy, thick nigger'. In some Arab countries where the ITV commentary was being relayed, the tirade was clearly audible. Atkinson was fired. Unfairly, Jimmy Hill argued in an interview with the *Independent*, 'In that context, you wouldn't think that words like nigger were particularly insulting: it would be funny. Without meaning to insult any black men, it's us having fun. What about jokes about my long chin? I mean, nigger is black – so we have jokes where we call them niggers because they're black. Why should that be any more of an offence than someone calling me chinny?' Any other presenter would have lost his job on the spot after such disturbed observations. Hill was generously forgiven, however. By then, viewers had long stopped taking him seriously.

There are not too many incisive things Hill can tell you about the current state of English football, but its past is another matter. Despite his high profile, surprisingly few people know of the major changes and developments he has personally brought about. Without Hill, English football – and football around the world – would look very different today. Up until a few years ago they used to call him 'Mr Football' in Britain, because he alone has done everything: Jimmy Hill has spent time as player, manager, chairman, president, referee and television presenter. No single Englishman has been responsible for more football innovations.

But let's start at the beginning.

Jimmy Hill was born on 22 July 1928 in Balham, South London, into modest circumstances. His father was a milkman. When he was twenty-one, Jimmy signed his first professional contract with Second Division Brentford, in the west of the capital. He remembers that in 1951 his side was invited by the Dutch football association to play a friendly against the national side. 'It was a 1–1 draw in Amsterdam. These days the result between the teams would probably be different. Hehehe!'

That same year, he played in front of 80,000 spectators in the Berlin Olympic Stadium as a member of a London XI. The match against a selection of Berlin-based players also ended 1–1. 'A very diplomatic result,' Hill chuckles. 'There was a huge dinner afterwards. We wondered why there was a free seat next to each of us. Then these blonde German girls were brought in. It was a good evening for Anglo-German relations. Hehehe!'

At Brentford he became a representative of the players' union, 'because I was the one who could read, write and add up'. He earned seven pounds a week as a striker, about £70 in today's money. That was for the winter, i.e. the actual playing season; during the summer break, it was common practice to pay less. Hill went to his coach and made him agree to a pay rise for the summer from five to six pounds. 'I told him that I was just as good a player in summer as in winter. Hehehe!'

In 1953, Hill moved to Fulham where he played until the end of his career in 1961. His record shows a total of 277 games and forty-one goals. He is still proud of having scored five goals in an away game against Doncaster – a league record. He was only booked once in twelve years as a professional footballer, and even that was unjustified, he says: 'The referee blew incorrectly for a throw-in against me. I wanted to know what I had done wrong, and he booked me for dissent. I sent a letter of complaint to the Football Association, but never got a reply.'

Hill did not become famous for his achievements on the pitch, but as a revolutionary and a class warrior after the end of his active career. As chairman of the players' union he pushed through the abolition of the maximum wage. Football League regulations had prevented professionals from earning more than twenty pounds per week (about £200 today). 'It was a feudal system,' Hill says. 'Firstly, there was a wage cap. Secondly, the clubs retained the rights to players after their contracts had expired and could force them to re-sign for less. There was no possibility of changing clubs. Those who didn't want to sign were forced to stick around anyway – without getting paid.'

Six weeks after his election as chairman of the players' union in 1956, Hill had to defend six Sunderland players who had been accused of accepting bonuses and backhand payments. This practice was as widespread in the post-war years as it had been in the 1870s and 1880s, the era of shamateurism. The Sunderland case showed just how absurd the maximum wage rule was. Hill collected the signatures of 250 players who admitted taking home more than the permissible twenty pounds per week. There was no indictment.

In spite of this, the Football League and the club chairmen dug their heels in and defended the status quo. Hill gradually succeeded in convincing the public of the injustice of the regulations. When the players' union, now called the Professional Footballers Association, threatened a strike in January 1961, the cigar-smoking president of the Football League, Joe Richards, finally gave in. Behind the scenes the government had been exerting pressure: the electorate was not to be deprived of their favourite pastime on Saturdays.

The maximum wage was scrapped and the employment relations were liberalised. Although the clubs continued to hold the rights to players after contracts had expired – it was not until Jean-Marc Bosman's appeal to the European Court of Justice in 1995 that footballers won complete freedom of employment – those who wished to move clubs could now appear before a neutral tribunal which would set the transfer figure. Players could no longer be tied to their old clubs without receiving a salary.

Did you receive any 'Sicilian message' from club presidents, did you find dead fish in your letterbox, Mr Hill? 'Not at all. Hehehe. It was a very hard but relatively fair struggle. The other side realised that they had no chance of winning. My boss at Fulham was a man called Tommy Trinder. He was an entertainer by profession, a stand-up comedian. He was able to negotiate his own appearance fee, so why should it have been any different for footballers? He had no answer to that.'

After this victory Hill was cheered each time he touched the ball. At the time the public and the media saw the conflict as a typical dispute between employers and employees and obviously took the side of the 'workers'. Jimmy Hill, the man who had effectively cleared the way for million-pound salaries, was hailed as a true working-class hero. Ironically he never did enjoy the new-found riches for players on a personal level. In March 1961 he badly injured his knee once more, and his career as a player was over.

Liberalisation of the labour market usually weakens the influence of unions, but the PFA has remained an institution with a lot of political clout. Its boss, Gordon Taylor OBE, is ever present to help defend footballers who misbehave in the hotel after an away game, or who 'forget' to appear at a drugs test, as Manchester United's Rio Ferdinand did in September 2003. The English newspapers do not particularly like Taylor, but are nevertheless thankful for the copy he reliably delivers. When, in October 2003, the English national side entertained the ridiculous idea of going on strike to protest against

Ferdinand's exclusion, they naturally received words of encouragement from Taylor. The sixty-four-year-old works hard for his protégés. With an annual salary in excess of £1 million he is the best-paid union leader in Britain, if not the world.

'When I read that players are now earning £120,000 per week I find it hard to believe what I have done,' Hill says, leaning back in a bright armchair with a floral pattern. Although in town to play tennis, he is wearing a green tie with the small blue emblem of Coventry City, where he began as a manager in summer 1961. Hill led the nondescript Third Division club from the Midlands into the First Division 'with innovative training techniques', as it says in his autobiography. When asked about these ingenious methods, Hill talks about cheap transfers and great camaraderie in the team. There never was a real secret to his success, he admits.

His ideas for marketing the club, on the other hand, were absolutely groundbreaking. Without being necessarily conscious of the fact at the time, he invented modern marketing strategies and fan events in the 1960s. Under his direction, a football club developed into a brand for the first time. As soon as he became manager he gave the team a new, sky-blue strip. The old, rather unglamorous nickname 'The Bantams' was replaced by 'The Sky Blues'. Hill also wrote a new club anthem, the 'Sky Blues Song'. At Highfield Road, and more recently at the Ricoh Arena, the ditty is still sung today. Hill organised the Sky Blues Express, a special train that took fans to away games. One of the three new stands was baptised 'Sky Blue Stand'. Of course – as is more often than not the case in England – there was a lot of alcohol involved as well. 'Back then I wasn't yet thinking about merchandising, but I wanted fans to identify more closely with the club,' Hill recalls. He leans forward in his chair. There is a satisfied glint in his eyes. 'On Christmas Day in 1961, we invited youngsters under sixteen to a small party with the players, with soft drinks and crisps. We thought about a hundred would turn up, but 670 children stayed behind after the game. The players had to sign autographs for three hours without pause. I went to the bar, brought back huge quantities of beer, and made sure that their glasses were never empty for long. They didn't notice that the party went on for several hours.' Hill is beside himself with laughter. 'I said, "Oh my God! What have I done here, again?" Hehehe.'

Coventry, which was almost totally destroyed by the Luftwaffe during the war, was booming – the car manufacturer Talbot was having its golden years – and City, thanks to Hill's ideas, was considered a cool club, a club for young people. From 1962 a DJ played music at Highfield Road on Sky Blues Radio, to entertain the fans before the match. 'There were no seats then,' Hill says, 'so the fans arrived at the stadium hours before the match to secure the best spots. Before kick-off they all used to get bored standing in the rain.' Hill arranged for school orchestras and military bands as entertainment. Gymnastic groups appeared, and girls played hockey. ('Once, and never again. Afterwards the players complained about the damage to the pitch. Hehehe.') Human pyramids piled up on moving police motorcycles. Occasionally the manager himself would ride around the pitch on a horse. 'The idea was to make the afternoon as enjoyable as possible for people. We couldn't afford the best players, so we had to think of another way.'

The Coventry model soon became much copied. Anybody who attended a Bundesliga game in the late seventies or early eighties will shudder at the memory of similar high-class shows. As soon as the clubs realised they could make a lot of money out of selling sausages before the game and at half-time, stadium entertainment fell out of fashion again.

Highfield Road had the first electronic scoreboard in England. On 6 June 1965, an away game (against Cardiff City) was shown live for the first time inside a stadium. That same year Coventry took part in a European tournament sponsored by Rover, which included a game against Kickers Offenbach. Prime Minister Harold Wilson gave his personal blessing to the trip – one had to think of exports, after all. Hill had intuitively recognised the marketability of English football.

Shortly before the start of the 1966–67 season, Coventry's debut in the First Division, Hill surprised fans by announcing he was moving to television. From 1968 he produced a football programme called *The Big Match* as head of sports for London Weekend Television. At the 1970 World Cup in Mexico, the independent broadcaster ITV got better viewing figures than the BBC for the first time. Hill had the idea of putting together a group of pundits – managers and players – for a discussion before and during the matches. No one had done this before. From today's perspective, the idea of inviting 'gurus and ex-gurus', as Rudi Völler would call these experts thirty-five years later, into the studio seems, like most of Hill's flashes of inspiration, astonishingly mundane. Perhaps it is always like that with good ideas: once they are implemented it is hard to believe that there was ever a time before they existed.

Hill returned to Coventry in 1980 and became their chairman. He installed the first under-soil heating in the league ('The technology came from Holland – hehehe – from potato farming!'). For the sponsor's sake he contemplated changing the club's name to Coventry Talbot FC. At the time, advertising on shirts was not yet permitted.

His time in office lasted less than three years. The club had put half a million dollars into a risky joint venture with the American Football League and soon had to write the money off. A highly modern training complex and club centre also proved over-ambitious. Hill had made enemies on the board. But it was another pioneering idea that ultimately cost him his job.

At the time, hooliganism was a very serious problem, at Coventry, too. Hill thought the solution was obvious: in 1981, he had Highfield Road converted into the first all-seater stadium in England. With this innovation, Coventry was too far ahead of the times. The fans protested vehemently against the disappearance of the terraces and gradually stayed away. In 1983, shortly before Hill's departure, the average crowd had dropped to 10,000. Two years later the seats were ripped back out of the Kop stand, which, just like its namesake at Anfield, is named after the Battle of Spion Kop in the Boer War. Hill's foresight would not be proved justified until 1990 when, in the wake of the Hillsborough disaster, the Taylor Report recommended that all-seater stadiums should be made compulsory.

All his historic achievements pale into insignificance, however, against his greatest and most important success. In England only very few people are aware – and in the rest of the world practically nobody knows – that Jimmy Hill invented the three-points-for-a-win rule.

At the beginning of the seventies the Isthmian League, an amateur league of clubs in and around London, came to Hill's consultancy firm with a big problem. The crowds were getting smaller and smaller. 'I proposed a few reforms,' Hill says. 'One of these was the three-point rule.' He had had the idea a long time before. 'As a player and then a manager I had noticed that many spectators went home in the final minutes, because often nothing more would happen on the pitch. If it was 0–0 or 1–1 the teams didn't want to take any more risks: it wasn't worth squandering everything for the second point. Matches would peter out. Fear played a part.'

Football ought to be different, Hill thought, more like theatre. 'The final act is always the best because it's when something happens or the leading star makes an appearance. Then you go home happy. The final act is what the audience remembers.' Hill imagined that a third point for victory might just entice teams to have another go right before the end and so send all their men forward. The Isthmian League took the plunge. A cigarette manufacturer was acquired as a new sponsor, and in 1974 the Rothmans League became the first competition in the world to play under the new rules. Several small leagues adopted the system over the following years. In 1981, Hill won over the Football Association and the Football League. Since the 1981–82 season England has been playing according to *his* points rule; the whole world signed up in 1994.

'Before, football had been getting a bit boring,' Hill recalls. 'Teams played very defensively. Thank God all that changed again.' English football, boring? Maybe compared with today's fast-paced, technically improved Premier League. But the judgement needs qualification. Whether football is seen as boring or not is principally a question of expectations. And in England these were, and still are, simply extraordinarily high.

In *Football Since the War: A Study in Social Change and Popular Culture* (1974), Chas Critcher is critical of the fact that by the time of the 1966 World Cup victory under coach Alf Ramsey the game's tactics had evolved from 4-2-4 to 4-3-3 ' to the ultra-defensiveness of 4-4-2'. 'The basic determinant of the choice of tactics was fear: the need to sacrifice long-term considerations of the game itself, to the prospects of immediate success.' For Critcher, a sociologist at the influential Centre of Contemporary Cultural Studies in Birmingham, this tendency towards defensive tactics proved that capitalism had permeated football entirely. 'The functionalism of post-Ramsey tactics is part of the cultural production of a society in which all activities are subjected to the same laws of financial security, immediate productivity and cultural conservatism.' Critcher did not exclude the possibility that tactics might change again in the future, or develop in a different direction. But he could not predict that precisely those commercial factors he deemed responsible for the decline of the beautiful game would later demand the renaissance of attacking, entertaining football. Like many on the left, he underestimated the ability of the system to change and adapt.

From a purely economic point of view, Hill's three-point reform of 1981 was simply a specific response to the football of the sixties and seventies which, for the general public, had become 'too functional'. A decade later it redeemed the rest of the football world from the worst excesses of *catenaccio*, and heralded the rise of the game to become mankind's favourite form of entertainment across the globe.

The contrast between the pure ideal of the sport and a football industry guided solely by financial interests is a major theme of football coverage; most conflicts between fans and clubs can comfortably be reduced to this dichotomy. The dialectic sometimes breaks down, however, when it comes to the question of English football's appeal as a product. Jimmy Hill has always openly been both a card-carrying capitalist and a genuine football lover. It is no accident that the man who shamelessly opened the floodgates to commerce, almost selling his club's name to a car manufacturer, also had the crucial idea of how the game could be made more beautiful, more exciting and better. The optimisation of football as a product was driven by a purist. It sounds ironic and contradictory, but it is perfectly logical. For all the lip service the English game pays to the past, people have always been quick to break with much-vaunted tradition if this was deemed necessary – and profitable.

Earlier than anywhere else, clubs in Britain became companies. Tottenham Hotspur floated on the stock market in 1983. Inevitably, a dual brand-consciousness developed among those involved: a consciousness of one's own brand as club or organisation, and that of the wider 'English Football' brand. The FA really mean it when they say that they are the custodians of the game. As a foreigner, you can't help but admire that the overwhelming majority of football fans seem united by a common concern for the well-being of the sport, despite all their rivalries. There is a strong, continual debate about how football can be protected from damaging influences, and how it can be made more exciting. This collective desire corresponds almost exactly to the modern commercial demands of making the product as telegenic and spectacular as possible. That is one of the secrets of English football's triumphant march across the globe. In the figure of Jimmy Hill, the game recognised thirty years ago that the needs of the adrenalin-addicted customers were best satisfied when the football was felt to be at its purest and most honest.

'I ought to have put a copyright on the three-point rule,' Hill laughs. 'The FA got it from me completely for free.' Yet the Premier League, always concerned about its public appeal, were pondering a new points system not long ago. In 2005, some club presidents wanted to see four points awarded for an away win. The reasons for the initiative were the same as in the seventies: the 'tendency for teams to opt for safety-first football, deploying only one forward in a cautious attempt to avoid defeat, was producing too much dull play, leaving fans frustrated', the *Observer* complained in May 2005. The strategy of going into away games with a 4-5-1 formation – not exactly a revolutionary tactic, you might think– was then a particular thorn in the side for club bosses. '4-5-1 is understandable,' a particularly pessimistic club chairman was quoted as saying in the *Observer*. 'It may help them pick up more points than they might otherwise have got and increase their chances of staying up, but it's often not exciting . . . it cannot be good for the Premier League in the long run.'

Hill does not think much of a rule change, though. 'I think the balance is right. After all, football should not be a strange game where nobody can remember the points system any more. Suddenly you'd have twenty-one points per game, one for every goal . . . No, I think the three points are correct; the balance is right.'

An afternoon with Jimmy Hill, with tea and cakes, comes to an end; the tennis court is calling. There's so much more we could have talked about: 'The Chin' has a view on everything and everybody. In May 2005 he told the *Guardian* that if he were Prime Minister he would immediately dissolve Parliament and give twenty businessmen the job of solving the country's problems. He also misses the old politeness on the roads. 'Is there anything lovelier than raising your hand and letting someone through? A civilised act like that makes the journey far more pleasant . . .'

But he has to get one last, big idea off his chest. 'There's one suggestion that I've never been able to push through, unfortunately: ex-professionals ought to be referees. That's so important. And so obvious. I have not the slightest doubt that the game would be much better for it. Of course you can't make good referees out of 2,600 professionals. But twenty could be exceptional referees.'

But why would they spend every Saturday and Sunday getting insulted?

'The problem is not that the players don't want to do it. It's simply that they're not being encouraged. You see, the authorities are worried that if only professionals were allowed to officiate in the top matches, then normal people wouldn't want to be referees any more. A million people play in this country every week; every ref is needed . . . It's not that simple, the whole thing.'

Hill, of course, has experience in this area. When a linesman was injured in an Arsenal–Liverpool match in September 1972, Hill rushed down to the touchline from his commentary spot and took the flag. He had a referee's certificate, naturally. Without him the game would have had to be abandoned: there were no replacement officials at the time.

'I'm afraid I didn't get anywhere with my idea about referees,' he smiles, rubbing his chin. Time for tennis. 'Is that enough? Have you got what you wanted? Oh good. Cheerio! And good luck.'

CHAPTER 6

Music, Fashion, Football:
The Holy Trinity

There are people in Britain with a sense of aesthetics who are convinced that Manchester United fully deserved their victory in the 1999 Champions League final. Not because the Red Devils were the better team. The theory goes that the Bavarians simply did not show the European Cup enough respect. Anybody who shuffles around the Nou Camp pitch like Carsten Jancker and co. in blue/red tracksuits, white socks and Adilettes (Adidas's plastic sandals) cannot be surprised if fate later strikes back. The United players were, of course, wearing bespoke Versace suits before kick-off. For the successful FA Cup final the Saturday before, Prada had been the outfitter.

In England it is a widespread belief that people who look like winners win more often. If you can't beat them, at least look as if you can. This attention to appearance might be seen as superficial, but in England they understand it is really about communication. The huge significance of fashion in English society is due to a class system that is much more pronounced than in most European countries. Strong contrasts sharpen the eye for differences. Clothing is important because it signifies where you come from, who you are, and who you want to be. Only the very rich can afford to dress like poor people. For the rest of the masses, pride and ambition dictate that you should look as smart as possible. In illustrations from the late nineteenth century one can see that the young hoodlums, already referred to back then as hooligans, placed great value on dressing elegantly.

What does this have to do with football? Everything. Because for more than a century football has been the sport of the English working class. Thus, the same rules of engagement apply. As recently as the 1970s English footballers would not celebrate being awarded a professional contract by going down the pub, but with a visit to the tailor: a bespoke suit was an unmistakable sign that you had made it. And 'you had it made'.

Professionals have to travel to matches in suits because they are representing their club. A suit is an apparatus for creating posture: it forces you to stand up straight with your chest puffed out. Even the footballers at Bangers and Mash FC in the lowest London pub league would not dream of turning up to the cup final against Pissed United without jacket and trousers. (Their WAGS would wear cocktail dresses.) When professionals appear at cup finals at Wembley, the identities of the suit designers are announced weeks in advance. Manchester United's FA Cup victory against Liverpool in 1996 has entered the history books as the 'white suits final'. The Reds wore ill advised cream Armani suits. The actual game (1–0, Cantona) has long been forgotten.

Football is always a question of style because football is pop. In Germany, some people proclaim, somewhat sniffily, that the Bundesliga has become part of today's hedonistic culture (*Spassgesellschaft*). It is easy to forget that it was always thus in the game's spiritual homeland. 'Music, fashion, football. The holy trinity of pop culture,' Paolo Hewitt and Mark Baxter write in *The Fashion of Football*.

The history of pop culture since the Second World War is the history of its inventors – young English working-class people – and it was played out in the stadiums as much as in clubs and concerts. Subcultures were bred in and around football grounds that had a long-lasting influence on teenage fashion – and sometimes on that of the footballers, too – throughout the whole world.

David Beckham, the first global pop star in football boots, had to be a working-class Englishman. It could only happen here. The son of a kitchen-fitter from Leytonstone developed style-consciousness and a sense for the perfect pose thanks to his surroundings.

It has always been essential for English football heroes to cut a good figure off the pitch. Bobby Moore, the captain of the 1966 World Cup-winning side, was not merely admired for his outstanding talent, but also for his stylish fashion sense. He took his cue from the 'mods', the 'modernists' – young Londoners who in the mid-sixties discovered the looks and sounds of American jazz and soul artists, as well as Italian motor scooters. During their lunch breaks they swallowed amphetamines in Soho clubs. Moore wore tight-fitting three-button suits, thin ties and cashmere jumpers; his mother ironed the laces of his football boots. The sixties was the decade of Swinging London, the Beatles and the Stones – England's decade. And Moore was one of its heroes: modern, cool, controlled and spotless. Elegance and cleanliness were his watchwords. His club, West Ham, became the epitome of elegant football – after the final whistle, too. Mike Summerbee of Manchester City once described him as the 'only man I knew who could get out of the bath dry'.

After England had won the World Cup final against Germany at Wembley, a single thought went through Moore's mind as he made his way to the presentation ceremony: would his slightly dirty hands soil the Queen's brilliant-white gloves?

'Mooro' later became a gentleman's outfitter and designed a leather jacket collection which was sold in Harrods, the luxury department store. The tabloid papers published endless reports about his huge house in Chigwell on the edge of London, his French maid, his designer suits. Moore even went to a manicurist. For a professional footballer that was no less extraordinary back then as Beckham's painted nails proved thirty-five years later.

George Best went further. From 1966 girls ran screaming after the Manchester United midfielder in the streets. Best, a Northern Irishman, was technically the best player the English league had ever seen. His popularity exceeded anything that had gone before. He looked dazzling, drove the most beautiful cars, and wore cooler clothes than the leading pop stars. Jackets and fine trousers, but never suits or ties. He was an individualist and rebel, a counter-cultural icon. Ray Davies of the Kinks honoured him with the song 'Dedicated Follower of Fashion'.

Best opened his own fashion boutiques in Manchester, principally so that he could chat up female customers. He was called the 'fifth Beatle' but was actually more the British equivalent of Elvis: a young man blessed with an astonishing talent who could not cope with his own fame, and simply drank away a large chunk of his career. An anti-hero with a self-destructive streak.

At the beginning of the seventies, when Best would go whole weeks without turning up for training and preferred to spend Saturdays in bed with young actresses rather than travelling to away games, Chelsea were known for playing the most beautiful football. And for wearing the best kit. The two were directly related, former Chelsea midfielder Alan Birchenall recalls: 'We had an unbelievably modern jersey, made out of thin nylon. You felt like an Italian in it. And that's how we played, too. We were technically so good that the other teams would get angry. They called us arrogant. If you play like that then of course you've got to look the part off the pitch, too. If you see a boring side, you can bet that the boys have no idea of fashion. If you see a team that plays brilliantly, then they often look the bollocks.' Apparently, the boys at Chelsea would dress especially fancily for games against the square hard men of Leeds United, just to wind up their archenemy.

Leeds were successful with their cynical football; Chelsea were the capricious, diva-like Hollywood side of their time. The Stones were regular visitors; honorary member Richard Attenborough dragged all sorts of American film stars to Stamford Bridge. In the Abramovich era the club is making every effort to revive this trendy image, as it is good for business. In an interview in the stadium's blue offices, chief executive Peter Kenyon explained to me that 'the Chelsea brand' will align itself with young people, fashion and music. 'All these things signify London. And Chelsea is London.' Perhaps no other top English club possesses so much popular cultural capital that is yet to be spent.

Unlike in football, the boundaries between heroes and also-rans in the world of popular music are substantially more permeable. Haircut, clothes, appearance are the only things teenagers can control themselves, and around the King's Road the youth were not content with merely copying the styles of the stars. They invented their own. Little of this is in evidence today. But you can still hear it in West London – the faint echo of the 1960s.

Chelsea against Bayern Munich, March 2005. Five minutes before kick-off, as ever at Stamford Bridge, a rousing reggae instrumental creaks out of the stadium's loudspeakers. The crowd claps along to the beat and fills the breaks in the riff with cries of 'Chelsaaah!' In the press box, the reporters who have travelled over from Germany glance at one another in disbelief and then start grinning. 'Yes, what a great song!' says one of them with the unavoidable irony of his profession; another one moves his fingers in the air, pretending to play the Hammond organ. Their conclusion? Only these crazy Englishmen could play such a weird, drugged-out song.

These German reporters do not mean to be condescending, they simply do not know better. From their own grounds they are used to 'Zillertaler Hochzeitsmarsch' (an insufferable oompah tune), *Star Wars*, OTT soundtracks from Jerry Bruckheimer films, or even the latest naff offering from Sarah Connor (don't ask) or Mr President (don't ask). The best they can hope for is Queen's 'We Will Rock You', or Tina Turner's 'Simply the Best'.

The song they play at Chelsea, however – and have been playing for far longer than most fans can remember – is 'Liquidator' by the Jamaican band The Harry J. Allstars. It was released in 1969 on the famous Trojan label in London, and was a top-ten hit. Still a good little number, but on the Fulham Road it is much more than that: a small piece of history, ritually celebrated in the family-friendly, pacified environs of Stamford Bridge to keep the memory alive. The memory of the spirit of '69; of Chelsea's past as a skinhead club.

The skins of the late 1960s had hardly anything in common with the bomber-jacket-wearing neo-Nazis you see on television. The vast majority of them were not racists but reggae-lovers; their natural enemies were not black immigrants but long-haired hippies. They wore American college shirts, brightly polished brogues and tight-fitting mohair suits in dark, iridescent colours. In *The Way We Wore*, his autobiographical book about the history of urban fashion in post-war London, Robert Elms, a fan of the west London side Queens Park Rangers, describes this radical subculture as a reaction to the hippy movement: 'a million miles away from the Chelsea flower-power show and arty happenings, [the younger hard nuts on the council estates] shaved their nuts and sharpened up their wardrobes. Like the predominant architectural style of the time, when unadorned, strictly functional blocks were springing up everywhere to house lumpen masses, we were about to witness the age of sartorial brutalism. And all too often there was the behaviour to go with it.' Historically, only prisoners and soldiers wore their hair this short. It was precisely this hard look that the skins cultivated.

Elms thinks it is ironic that the sixties are generally described as colourful years of love, mind-expanding drugs and anti-Vietnam demonstrations; in his view, history-writing has been kidnapped by middle-class kids. Where he lived there was 'fighting and football, not peace and love'.

The former editor of *The Face*, the most important style bible of the eighties and nineties, sees the skins of 1969 as modern incarnations of the London dockworkers from the seventeenth century. Back then these ruffians, who shaved their heads bald to avoid lice, and were scornfully described as 'roundheads', fought in the English Civil War on the side of the Protestants against the King and his long-haired Catholic knights.

There was no war for the 1960s generation of working-class kids to fight, however, and no army. National service had been abolished. So they created their own army, their own uniform and their own ideology of violence. The defence of their own patch, always a fundamental aim of young members of the working class and football fans, became a sacred task. 'Skins were extremely defensive of their won territory. Each gang . . .

had its own area which it defended against other skins and non-skins,' Nick Knight writes in *Skinhead*. 'Territorial infringement' resulted in serious beatings.

In their martial appearance and behaviour characterised by toughness and aggressive masculinity, the sociologist John Clark recognised a subconscious attempt to preserve the values of the working-class community which were under great threat from social and industrial change. The battle the skins waged was a symbolic, rearguard battle without any real prospect of success. British neo-Nazis were easily able to make use of the violent and reactionary potential of the movement, and the scene was rapidly infiltrated to the core by right-wing extremists.

Travelling Chelsea and West Ham fans spread the look throughout England. Leicester fan Jim Ferguson remembers Chelsea skinheads coming to a game at Filbert Street in 1968. A week later there was the first sighting of skins in Leicester. 'Just as *Ready Steady Go!* had spread fashion nationwide, the London football fan now took over the role, taking his clothes and style to all the major cities,' Hewitt and Baxter write. *Ready Steady Go!* was the first pop music programme on British television. It brought Swinging London and the feel of the sixties to the screen.

By 1969 skinheads had become a national cult that had profoundly changed the atmosphere in the stadium. There was a dramatic rise in the readiness to use violence, and this in turn had an effect on fashion. Gear now had to be practical and as indestructible as possible. Doctor Marten shoes became popular, as did tight jeans and jackets made out of synthetic, tear-proof materials. Even the bald head took on a very functional significance: adversaries could not pull your hair in close combat.

There were even female skins. In Hewitt and Baxter's

book the Tottenham skin Keith Palmer raves about the 'Tottenham Skin Girls', a group of twenty-five young women who drove the boys at White Hart Lane crazy with their Ben Sherman shirts, mini-dresses and black tights. When Palmer tentatively dared to approach them the girls gave him a sound thrashing.

There is a twinkle in John King's eyes as he recalls the days when '500 Chelsea skins used to stir up the King's Road'. For the author of *The Football Factory*, a novel on a par with *Fever Pitch* and David Peace's *The Damned United*, it was precisely the club's naughty reputation that had such a huge attraction: 'As a young man, of course you wanted to go where you could smell a bit of danger.' Today, the King's Road smells of expensive perfumes worn by blonde women of an indeterminate age who hop from one antique shop to another in 4×4s.

In 1971–72, when the media became aware of the phenomenon, it was already past its peak. The political radicalisation and the accompanying police persecution had scared off the broad mass of fans; those skins who remained committed to the look turned into an ultra-violent minority. The bulk of the original skins had by then visibly distanced themselves by wearing 'more normal' clothes and haircuts.

English newspaper caricaturists still picture hooligans as skinheads today, even though they disappeared from the grounds for good more than twenty years ago. At Stamford Bridge and Molineux, Wolverhampton Wanderers' ground, 'Liquidator' is still a musical reminder of them. A few trappings from their uniform remain, too, albeit in a diluted form. You no longer see 'Docs' or braces, but there are still an awful lot of men with noticeably short hair. The 'number two cut', named after the second grade on electric hair clippers, is the universal, unmistakable mark of a 'real' English football fan. It is not only a convenient ruse to conceal hair loss – as seats are getting more expensive, the audience is getting older – but a warning sign. It is a haircut that says 'Watch yourself!' in bold letters. To this day, every Premier League player who fancies himself as a hard man or simply wants to feign real commitment shaves his head.

In the mid-1970s, punks took over from skins as picture-perfect trouble-makers. But this scene could not last long, either. The media, which was by now reacting faster to young people's trends, reported punk to death. Countless articles and television reports carried the style – born on the King's Road, not far from Chelsea's ground – to the outermost corners of the kingdom until suddenly every second British youngster was shuffling down the street wearing safety pins and bin liners. The anarchic philosophy was not compatible with the increasing uniformity of the mass movement. Punk got too big and ate itself.

At the same time, a totally new style of fashion gradually developed in the stands at Anfield in Liverpool. At first this went almost unnoticed, but more and more fans started to turn up in smart leisurewear made by Lacoste or Sergio Tacchini, and in trainers. It took time for someone to come up with a name for these strange characters. In the end they were called 'casuals'. They changed European fan culture and football itself.

Why Liverpool? London had always been at the forefront of fashion. But at the end of the 1970s the Scousers had one big advantage: they were travelling abroad. The Reds were by some distance the most successful English club in the European Cup, and the fans would bring back French and Italian sportswear brands from their many trips that people had not seen in England before. 'On the Monday before the 1981 European Cup final in Paris [against Real

Madrid] no Parisian sportswear shop would let you in if you looked at all English,' Peter Hooton recalls. 'Liverpool fans had nicked everything they had.' In 1981 Hooton founded *The End*, the first fanzine, which was chiefly devoted to terrace fashion.

The English papers and police authorities misunderstood the strange trend as some sort of camouflage. They explained the desire of football fans to dress like the gilded youth of Europe as a need for disguise. And it was of course true that without the obligatory scarves and colours, individuals were less hassled; hooligans could disappear unrecognised into the crowd before and after punch-ups because they were no longer identifiable as supporters.

But for the 'scallies' from Liverpool, this fashion stood for something else, something far more banal and important at the same time: they really wanted to look good. The city was under enormous pressure politically and socially. After Margaret Thatcher came to power and declared war on the unions, the heartland of the dockworkers and miners felt abandoned. In the media, the city was only ever portrayed as England's poorhouse and an enclave of unemployment. With their consumption of luxury goods put ostentatiously on show, the scallies signalled that they were not going to be deprived of their right to *la dolce vita*. Young unemployed men with no job were wearing yuppie leisurewear: it amounted to a cheery two-fingered salute to the establishment.

In 1979, after the Cup final between Arsenal and Manchester United at Wembley, the casuals' style took off in London, too. Sportswear shops opened up near many football stadiums. One of the best of these was Stuart's, around the corner from QPR's ground in Shepherd's Bush. 'On Friday afternoon before a game you would literally get queues of kids stretching up the Uxbridge Road desperate to hand over ludicrous amounts for specialist attire for sports they'd never dream of playing,' Elms writes.

The casual craze was effectively an extension of the battle zone. From now on your fashion gear was just as important as 'doing the business' in the streets. You had to look better than the enemy 'crews'. Those who did not have the money starved, stole or stripped somebody. The best items were taken from opposition fans. This practice was called 'taxing', and like all good youth trends it came to Germany a few years later, together with the corresponding fashion. Anybody who had the misfortune to travel alone at night in the Munich underground in the late 1980s may have surrendered their Best Company sweatshirt to Bayern hooligans with shaven heads, Adidas Torsion trainers and Diesel jeans cut above the ankles.

Elms writes, 'Football hooliganism, which was as much a facet of British youth's sometimes violent brilliance as any pop craze or fashion trend, was just one of the ways in which we were ahead of everybody else. Like mod, punk and new romantic, we invented it. By 1980, the terraces and the pubs and clubs around them were terrifying places where well-drilled, sharply attired firms left calling cards on their razor-cut victims . . . And just as Europeans picked up on punk, years after it emerged in London, but never quite got it right, never got any pop culture really right, so finally they also took to football hooliganism, the English sickness.'

In the era of the casuals, football violence reached a new climax. Local and regional animosities were played out to extremes; the eighties became synonymous with out-of-control football violence. And there was no doubt that the lovers of luxury brands owed a debt that needed discharging. With shopping and fashion-awareness traditionally seen as a feminine concern, the potential deficit in masculinity had to be compensated for by even more physical machismo. The social disparity between supporters of different clubs also came to the fore. From the stands, London casuals would wave banknotes at less affluent northerners, or show off their designer underwear. The new formula was: hardness = style + power to spend, the sociologist Simon Frith writes.

Interestingly, books written by former casuals are full of anecdotes about tasty encounters that never came to blows because one side had had too clear a fashion advantage. Elms describes an away game at Coventry during the 1983–84 season. 'Four hundred swells . . . are dressed. They have Diadora Gold or Adidas Forest Hills trainers, a few even sport Gucci loafers . . . Kappa tracksuits and Fiorucci jeans . . . The aim is to be one step ahead, to display your prowess, your spending power and your pace . . . Suddenly, they are confronted by the opposite numbers, a gang of Midland youth, blocking their path, looking for a confrontation . . . The two sides stand snarling at each other, rapidly eyeing the opposition up . . . Will it kick off, who will throw the first blow, who will run?' Then the QPR boys spot a weakness. They've noticed that a few of the Coventry lads are wearing Fila trainers. 'My dog sleeps on Fila, my dog sleeps on Fila, la la la la' the Rangers fans start singing. Fila used to be cool in London, but that was last month. Instead of launching themselves at the Londoners in anger, the Coventry firm hesitate. '[They] started looking each other up and down, perusing their togs and looking closely at what Rangers were wearing. It dawned on them that they'd been outdone in the style stakes. You could see their faces drop and their will for the contest wane. As the desire for a fight seeped away, they slipped away, too. They'd been beaten and they knew it.'

In spite of the ubiquitous violence, 'casual' therefore hinted at the possibility of shifting the conflict to a second, symbolic level. Those who could prevail with style no longer needed to use their fists. Michael Jackson's 'Beat It' clip told a similar story at the very same time. Two rival gangs – one are Rockers, the other Soul Boys, or American casuals, if you want – are about to slug it out in a backyard. But then they see Michael Jackson dancing. They drop their knives and dance along with him, united by the same choreography. United by pop.

Of course that is not quite what happened in Thatcher's England in the mid-eighties. It sadly needed an absolutely huge shock, the catastrophes of Heysel and Hillsborough, to bring about a fundamental rethink and a significant reduction in violence. It is unlikely, however, that the new policing measures and rebuilding of the stadiums at the end of the decade would have produced the much-vaunted renaissance of football if the casuals had not inadvertently created part of the necessary precondition. Thanks to their efforts, football had transformed into a lifestyle, to be reported on in *The End* and other fanzines with stacks of wit and humour. The emphasis on smartness of attire and thought – the prominence of style and originality – had opened up a rational vent for rivalries and made the sport compatible with a more peaceful type of entertainment. Through the fan culture of the casuals, football was cultivated from the bottom up. From now on there was at least the theoretical possibility of fighting solely with fashion and chants. For the majority, verbal and stylistic contests soon replaced actual brawls.

Through warehouse parties and raves, football fans came into contact with the fashionable drug Ecstasy. The rush of endorphins did not lead to peace breaking out all over England, but there was certainly a significant decline in aggression. Casuals founded successful pop groups such as the Farm (Liverpool) and the Stone Roses (Manchester); in London, a football-pop magazine and record label called

Boy's Own appeared. Andrew Weatherall and Terry Farley, two of its creators, are world-famous music producers today. Football became fashionable, cool and hip. England's national side went into the 1990 World Cup with the fine 'World in Motion' by Manchester's New Order, whereas Germany were crashing 'Überm Brenner' with Austrian naff-meister Udo Jürgens at the steering wheel. (It would take us a few more years to wake up to football's pop-cultural potential.) A sense of carnival started ruling at many grounds. Supporters were suddenly bringing blow-up bananas, animals and even paddling pools to the games. The ability to fight was severely limited with a plastic palm tree on your head.

Even hardcore hooligans such as West Ham's 'Inter City Firm' realised that in the new, emerging media society it was more profitable and safer in the long run to shift their activities to a commercial level. In 1988 the ICF ran its own merchandising and was advising television companies; hooligans became businessmen, party organisers and novelists. With fewer actual riots in and around the stadiums, nostalgic hooligan autobiographies filled the void. The success of Nick Hornby's *Fever Pitch* proved that football was now an acceptable passion for the middle class.

It was now impossible to pick out the casuals in the ground as we'd all become casuals long before. Europe's pedestrian zones are populated by young people in trainers, sweatshirts and baseball caps, unaware that their style's roots lie in north-west England.

Not everybody was happy about the rapid gentrification of football though. In the provinces, especially, they stubbornly refused to accept the paradigm shift. On the contrary, those firms were even proud of being the last blemishes on the face of a sport that, on the whole, had scrubbed up really nicely. There was also a cultural backlash in the mid-nineties, an anti-intellectual reaction to the new mainstream. Magazines and television programmes suddenly celebrated the 'New Lad', the unreconstructed male who loved beer, tits and football. The big pop feud between Oasis, the band of unemployed men from Manchester who furnished 'new laddism' with its soundtrack, and their arch-rivals from London Blur, with their ironic art-student Britpop, was symbolic of this division. Both bands wanted to write the official song for Euro 96. The organisers shied away from making this hugely political choice and ultimately settled for the reassuringly bland Lightning Seeds from Liverpool, and the comedy duo of Skinner and Baddiel.

All the sense of irony inherent in this attack on the new, sensitive man of the early nineties was lost by the time it reached the stands. England defender Graeme Le Saux was routinely called a homosexual because he had outed himself as a *Guardian* reader. When playing away from home, David Beckham would be asked by ten thousand blokes whether his wife preferred unusual sexual practices.

Oh yes, Beckham. Around the turn of the millennium, 'the first postmodern footballer' (Real Madrid president Florentino Perez) was declared by journalists and academics, not wholly without reason, to be a phenomenon. His appeal transcended the sport. Beckham stopped being famous for his skills on the pitch and became famous for his fame. *The Face* photographed him in a blatantly homoerotic fashion shoot as the nation's blood-smeared messiah. Chinese girls who had never seen a football match in their lives idolised him. After his transfer to Spain in July 2003, Real Madrid sold 8,000 football shirts in the first weekend alone. 'Becks', the metrosexual son of a kitchen-fitter, a man with Hebrew and Indian letters tattooed on his arms, played along. He enthusiastically accepted his status as a gay icon, jetted to fashion shows straight after the final whistle and used summer breaks to introduce the Beckham luxury brand to America with his wife Victoria, alias 'Posh Spice', in anticipation of a move to the LA Galaxy.

Beckham's astonishing appeal helped to win football new markets and to establish it as a global form of entertainment. Only once he had left for Spain did the realisation dawn on the English that his influence on the sport itself had probably been overestimated. The gulf between his image and his actual achievements on the pitch had become 'as wide as the Grand Canyon' (*Süddeutsche Zeitung*) by the time England were heading for their customary quarter-final exit against Portugal in Gelsenkirchen. South Africa in 2010 might offer one last chance of redemption, but chances are that Becks will forever remain a well-dressed but empty promise. In the last four major tournaments in France, Holland/Belgium, Japan/South Korea and Portugal, his performances simply bore no relation to the unbelievable hype surrounding him.

The completely unnecessary sending-off in the last-sixteen match against Argentina in the World Cup in France turned the young Spice Boy into a traitor to the national cause, and also threw up an uncomfortable question: what sort of man flicks his heel on to the thigh of an opposition player while lying on the ground? A powerful punch would have been much more forgivable than this tentative – in fact only insinuated – attack from behind. In 2000 he was an also-ran; in 2002 he was not properly fit and, worst of all, a bottler. In the second minute of stoppage time, shortly before the end of the first half against Brazil, he skipped over Roberto Carlos's challenge for fear of injury. The ball went via Ronaldinho to Rivaldo and then into David 'Safe Hands' Seaman's net. Had England's goalkeeper not managed to flap fatefully at a Ronaldinho free kick later in the match, Beckham would have been saddled with the chief blame for the defeat again. At the European Championship in Portugal he hit his penalty against the hosts so high over the bar it has still not come down. Again, he was patently not fit at that tournament; too many advertising appointments and parties in Madrid had robbed him of his energy during the season. No self-control, fear, lack of power and nerves: no England captain could be so unmanly.

This may be irrelevant to his Asian fans, but the English were disappointed. Theirs was not the only loss. Ultimately, Beckham has not quite managed to be the harbinger of a new age of football, in which the traditional mythology of excessive masculinity and the glorification of toughness would play a less prominent role. His new-found role as devoted elder statesman might have won him the sympathies of the fickle New Wembley crowd. But soon this collective amnesia will vanish in the wake of another nondescript big-game performance, and he will sadly have only confirmed the age-old prejudices: a fashion mouse does not have a lion's heart.

St George's hopes have meanwhile shifted to Wayne Rooney. The Liverpudlian is the anti-Beckham, an uncouth ne'er-do-well who spent eighteen months frequenting back-street brothels and who after a beer or two did not bother to look that closely. 'His conquests included a 48-year-old grandmother, a mother of six in a cowboy outfit and a girl in pink underwear,' crowed the *Sun*. Great fun, for £45 per hour. Unfortunately he found it difficult to publicly deny the story: Wayne was caught on CCTV, and also used to leave autographs instead of tips as a little 'thank you' for the treatment he had received. 'I shagged you on the 28 of December. Love, Wayne Rooney.' If you called Rooney a metrosexual to his face he would probably scratch his big head in bewilderment and then knock you down with a right hook just to be on the safe side. The police have had to break up the odd Rooney family event because of serious punch-ups. He proposed to Coleen in a Cadillac on a petrol station forecourt. Nice.

He is the king of chav. And they love him for it. With him, football takes a symbolic step back to where it came from, and where, when it comes down to it, it still feels most comfortable: on the street, where the air is pungent with regurgitated kebabs and urine, and men disappear into 'beauty salons' on the lookout for cheap sex.

Hero worship is subject to the laws of fashion, too, of course. It is dependent on success, and cyclical. Sometimes people want the bad boys, sometimes the good ones. The Holy Trinity of English youth will continue to exist, however. Football will always be part of popular culture, albeit in changed form. At the very top, the gentrification of the sport since 1990 has marginalised the traditional working-class public. The entry prices are increasing faster than the average income, and as a consequence the crowds are becoming older and more affluent. You cannot expect new fashion impulses from such a clientele. Today, fashion is increasingly being created from above, by footballers and other celebrities, and the fans, or customers, follow. New subcultures will surely continue to emerge here, as the English love nothing more than flocking together in constantly evolving little tribes. But the action will be far away from the lit-up stadiums, most probably in dark niches of rough areas of cities. And they will almost certainly have nothing whatsoever to do with football.

CHAPTER 7

Richard Burton and Elizabeth Taylor: The Love–Hate Relationship Between Football and the Press

It's September 2005, and English football is in crisis. Two bookmakers are already paying out bets put on Chelsea. Everybody else is out of the running. The Premier League – the plaything of a blue cat that became a monster thanks to Siberian oil. Sven Göran Eriksson's boys have just been humiliated by the Lower Division XI that is Northern Ireland, and are about to schlep themselves, tired out, to another disappointing World Cup. Hardly any other European team can boast so much individual talent; none utilises it so badly. There is no fire. No passion. No leadership. If it were up to Mr Ordinary on a Clapham omnibus the FA would have sacked the emotionless Swede long before the tournament and replaced him with an old-school English manager. Preferably someone who shouts a lot.

The cricketers are the beneficiaries of football's malaise. They have finally, after eighteen years, beaten the Australians in the prestigious battle for the Ashes and are the nation's darlings. Freddie Flintoff, a man with a hooligan haircut and minor weight issues, beams from the front page of every newspaper. He is the new Beckham. In December, the cricket heroes are named BBC 'Team of the Year'. There is no more talk of Liverpool, the triumphant winners of the Champions League.

Like all true lovers of the game, Henry Winter seems a bit unnerved about all this, a little resigned almost. Yet there is a mischievous smile on his lips and a clever twinkle in his eye. Winter is chief football writer for the *Daily Telegraph*, one of the most respected sports journalists in the country, and from a professional point of view he is quite pleased with the downtrodden mood. In a few minutes' time he is going to be interviewing Richard Scudamore, chief executive of the Premier League, about the current crisis. 'Newspapers are like stockbrokers,' he says, stirring his cappuccino. 'We make our money when share prices move up or down. They mustn't stay on the same level.' A bear market is good for business, in other words. Particularly in England, where football is considered to be in permanent decline, along with the whole country. In his essay 'Playing the Past: The Media and the English Football Team', Stephen Wagg argues that the England football team has long been seen as 'a metaphor for England itself. As Britain declined economically, shed its empire and faced up to a world dominated by two new superpowers, Fleet Street spoke as if a still great nation was being betrayed by the bunglers and shirkers who ran, or were, its football team.'

For the sport that was supposedly gifted to the world by the British Empire, status anxiety is almost unbearable. At the very top, the only way open to you is down. And downhill it has gone for English football, since long before the concept of a golden past had even been invented. In the late nineteenth century the amateurs bemoaned deteriorating moral standards in the wake of professionalism. Formations became ever more defensive. After the Second World War England were beaten by the US and Hungary. Crowds became smaller. By the sixties spectators were said to have been 'in revolt' against the disruption of 'the essence and flow of the game by deliberate fouls, perpetual dissent, feigned injuries and other forms of gamesmanship' (Critcher). England missed out on two World Cups in the seventies, then saw the rise of hooliganism, then the banishment from Europe. The Premier League boom, too, was a double-edged sword, naturally: it ushered in a new era of prawn sandwiches, roasting, unaffordable ticket prices and fourth-choice strips. 'For football as a genuinely popular cultural activity, the final whistle may already have gone,' Critcher wrote – more than thirty years ago.

Forty-odd years of hurt on the international stage have compounded this sense of unstoppable decay, the success of the Premier League and its clubs in Europe notwithstanding. The seminal role that foreign investment and personnel have played in this respect has left enough scope for concern, as has the appointment of Fabio Capello as England manager. 'We solve problems the only way we know – by throwing lots of money at them,' wrote Martin Samuel in *The Times* about the FA's choice, which he saw as a form of cheating.

The papers play up to these residual doubts brilliantly and keep the multi-layered neurosis alive. The inferiority complex of 'we are useless' is superimposed on an atavistic sense of natural supremacy – 'we can't even beat *this lot*'. This way, all bases are covered. Even when the Big Four are dominating the Champions League, the coverage tends to concentrate on the weaknesses of Spain and Italy, or on raw fear: will UEFA and FIFA try to knock the English clubs off their perch with some insidious bureaucratic initiative?

As Winter says, it is all about movement, a constantly evolving narrative. Newspapers deliberately write off teams, coaches or players so that their eventual rise can be even more dramatic; or suffocate a team under a blanket of superlatives until they can dance on its grave. In March 2009 the papers were wondering whether Ferguson's team was the best British side ever, only to report that they had been found out and were falling apart in the wake of two league defeats.

This is not about news; new mini-dramas have to be scripted and staged every single day. There is an awful lot of Christian symbolism involved as well. Players are forever 'falling from grace' only to 'redeem themselves' a bit later, if possible by bleeding, sweating and crying all over the holy shirt worn by crusaders a thousand years ago.

'There's no doubt that we've got the best and worst journalism in the world,' Winter says. 'Both of these are a consequence of the extraordinary competition.' The media cannot pull their punches here, their manner is as uncompromising as the footballers' on the pitch. In numbers alone they are in a league of their own; no other Western country is able to support this many newspapers. Ten national dailies and the London *Evening Standard*, the largest-circulation local paper in Europe, compete for readers with good, bad and ugly headlines. More than twelve million copies are sold every day. Then there are thirteen English Sunday papers with a total print run of thirteen million copies. The magnificent *Sunday Times*, with half a dozen colour supplements and twenty pages of sport, is so heavy that you have to throw away at least the children's and travel sections on the way home from the newsagent's, lest your arm fall off.

One of British society's most attractive features is the high regard it has for public discourse. The quality of political debate, from the tabloids all the way through to television, is easily more sophisticated than in Germany, and, I expect, than in most of Europe, too. To have a way with words is a strong cultural imperative. When at Arsenal, Jens Lehmann was thrilled to see that his young children were taught debating skills at their London schools, 'something we [Germans] would do only in our late teens'.

It is intriguing to note that Brits talk of 'taking' their favourite newspaper, not of 'reading' it. This turn of phrase reveals a more invasive, closer relationship to the medium. They take *The Times* or the *Sun*, just as they take their medicine or two sugars with their tea.

So this is a country that believes in the power of the word; that is why newspapers are so cherished, so demonised, so feared. But there's an alternative explanation, and it goes back to this island's dark pleasure in imagining itself as a sinking ship. The English might simply love newspapers because they love bad news so much.

The dailies and Sundays can be divided into three groups: tabloids are principally separated from the broadsheets; the mid-markets are a mixture of the two. There is a paper that specialises in betting, the *Racing Post*, but no specialist sports newspaper. The regular papers satisfy that particular need sufficiently; on Mondays and in Champions League weeks they will publish special football supplements as well. Monthly magazines such as *4-4-2* or *Champions* have an unenviable task in the face of all this competition. With their long lead times, they hopelessly straggle behind the up-to-date daily press who are also increasingly moving online, into real-time analysis. What is more, the few exclusive interviews that are to be had rarely appear in the monthlies' pages. They are to be found in the club magazines of Arsenal, Manchester United or Chelsea.

In comparison with their international counterparts, the English national newspapers enjoy truly extraordinary resources. Whereas in Germany even national papers such as the *Süddeutsche Zeitung* and the *Frankfurter Allgemeine Zeitung* resort to agency reports for some Bundesliga matches, in England a writer is sent to every Premier League fixture. The most important games are always covered by two or three journalists. The entire press corps even travels to the remotest corners of Europe to cover irrelevant away games on the last day of the Champions League group phase. Most of the Sundays come along for a couple of days, too, just in case. Something might happen, after all.

In London, you can go into a shop on Wednesday night at half past midnight and buy Thursday's paper with a detailed report of the previous evening's game, rounded off with two or three think pieces or columns, as well as the managers' quotes from the press conference. Germany's archaic employment laws make night shifts extremely costly, however. For all intents and purposes, national dailies like *Süddeutsche* really work to evening paper deadlines. Floodlit games only make it into the local edition. Serious analysis will only be written the next morning. If you want more than a simple match report for Wednesday's match, you will have to buy Friday's paper. It's a bizarre work mode and clearly unsustainable in times of Twitter.

In England, leading writers like Winter are on the road 300 days a year and are rewarded with Bundesliga 2-type salaries. When Harry Harris was employed as the chief columnist of the *Daily Express* he reportedly earned £300,000 per year. No German hack can come close to these figures. The rate of pay for one-off pieces is also about 50 per cent higher. At least it was before the pound tumbled like Cristiano Ronaldo in the opposition's penalty box. As a stringer, you can make a few hundred for a simple piece of information, or by coming up with a useful quote. Some foreign football journalists have earned more by selling player quotes to English papers than from their reports for their desks back home.

The fees may be lavish by continental standards, but the editorial teams are relatively small. One or two editors plan and copy-edit the texts, helped by sub-editors who will also come up with headlines. Only the writers write. Freelance journalists play practically no role here.

The 'number ones' (chief writers) on the paper lead charmed lives, and can expect to be invited to exclusive briefings by the England manager and players. For the journalists on the dailies who do not belong to this elite circle, however, each day is a struggle. A struggle with sports television and radio, both of which are more up to the minute; with the internet and the agencies; with the papers that are their direct competition, of course; and even with colleagues on the Sundays. They might be published by the same media company, but will mostly have completely independent editorial teams. Before the challenges of the internet forced papers to integrate across the platforms there was little or no exchange of information between the *Daily Telegraph* and *Sunday Telegraph*; no cooperation, only pressure.

'I've personally thrown SID [a German news agency] representatives out of England press conferences,' Winter says. 'It's not right if the quotes can appear on the wires a few hours later. Nobody needs to read your articles any more.' The English would not tolerate the sort of press conference that is usual in Germany – 'all-ins' without any special privileges and a live broadcast on television. Here, dailies and Sundays insist on interviewing players and managers separately. 'When they arrive here, foreign coaches have no idea what we're after,' says Rob Draper, football correspondent at the *Mail on Sunday*. 'They're not used to commenting on the same thing twice.'

The separate question-and-answer sessions are useful, however. After a Saturday match, for example, the dailies have scant interest in the game that has just finished and will ask about Tuesday's Champions League fixture, whereas the Sundays still need one or two quotes for their reports. At Champions League matches, this routine is repeated in the mixed zone, but the roles are reversed. The gentlemen of the Sundays now stand far away from the dailies to talk to footballers about the league match on the coming Sunday. No agencies and/or writers from the dailies are allowed near; after all, the quotes must remain fresh and unused until the weekend.

'We're like wolves. We keep quotes for days like morsels of food, so we can live off them in lean times,' Winter explains. When, for example, one Sunday Jens Lehmann expressed his displeasure at sitting on the bench, the newspapers, after consulting with one another, did not print his (relatively mild) criticism of Wenger until the following Tuesday. Nevertheless, the articles began with the words, '*Last night*, Lehmann slammed Wenger' to make it sound as if it were up-to-date news. Winter: 'Lines are activated at the push of a button, when there's not much going on, or if they fit the story well. I remember "David Beckham: I want to fly to the moon." The text began with, "Last night, Beckham said . . ." but in truth the quote was a few months old.' The tabloids also like to take excerpts from interviews that have been published abroad and sell them weeks later as news.

Surprisingly, it is not just competition between writers that is intense but also their collaboration. After press conferences the journalists, especially those from the tabloids, come together in the so-called 'press huddle' for an ad hoc debate. They put their heads together, then make a joint decision as to which 'lines' were the most important, and on the general direction of the piece. 'I already knew that it was like that,' confides a press spokesman for a northern English club, who would rather remain anonymous. Let us call him Peter Smith. 'But when I first saw grown men flocking together to settle on what they all should write the following day, I was shocked. It's always a strange scene. Normally there's one unofficial spokesman who will read out the "best" quotes, and then play around with them until the most sensational interpretation is possible. The others nod, and the following day an almost identical headline that bears little relation to the actual quote will appear across five papers. Either "Manager Joe Bloggs blasts Manager so-and-so" or "Manager Joe Bloggs slams the ref". To blast and to slam are the only verbs allowed. If there is nothing at all negative in the statement, the subs turn it into a "Manager Joe Bloggs backs player so-and-so". As if that were news.'

One might think that papers would value independence of thought and prefer to run somewhat more individual assessment. But the tabloid writer's self-preservation instinct is stronger than the courage to go his own way. If the *Sun* were to exaggerate a manager's remark out of all proportion to create an angle the *Mirror* had overlooked, the *Sun* journalist might get a little praise but his *Mirror* colleague would be looking at a roasting from his editor (not in the football player's sense of the word, it needs to be said). 'Colleagues have lost their jobs because they've missed a story,' says Martin Lipton, chief writer at the *Mirror*. The exchanges in the press huddle, and the collective adoption of a uniform line, avert this danger. The upshot: every molehill grows into K2 on the back page the next day.

'You want a splash that provokes a reaction in the reader,' Lipton says. 'They have to say "Fuck me!" when they see it. Men start reading the paper from the back, with the sports section, and a good back page can make the difference at the newsagent's.' Or a good headline. English subs have perfected the art of the witty headline. An unwritten law demands puns, which are sometimes so far-fetched (or bad) that even English people have trouble understanding them. Take GIVE US A KIESS (*Daily Star*) and BLUES' NEW SAHIN-SATION (*Mirror*). Supposedly, Wenger wanted to sign Nuremberg's Stefan Kiessling, and Chelsea were after Dortmund player Nuri Sahin. THE WALLY WITH THE BROLLY (*Daily Mail*) – Steve McClaren – was more straightforward, if perhaps a little below the belt. 'Our sports section has to have four rows of teeth,' demanded Frank Nicklin, sports editor at the *Sun* in the 1980s. All rival papers can do is escalate the tone. Next to these hyper-aggressive tabs, *Bild* reads like a memo from the local parish.

The artificial severity of many articles leads the media and footballers into a vicious circle. Managers and players are so wary of having their quotes wantonly misconstrued that they will either say utterly bland or irrelevant things or nothing at all. The lack of decent base material in turn forces journalists to sex up the banalities until they work as sensational splashes. 'The subs are under pressure to create the strongest headline the text can support,' Lipton says. 'They often push it too far. Most of our problems are down to the headlines. I often have to apologise for lines I haven't even written.' If managers feel they are being deliberately misquoted, a writer might get banned from a ground for several weeks. Over the years countless journalists have had to buy tickets and file copy from among the crowds. The papers do not take this exclusion lying down, however. They will Photoshop the photographs that accompany the match reports, blanking out the names of the sponsors.

All sides soon calm down again. But not Alex Ferguson.

The Scot can be unforgiving. He has repeatedly called sports desks to complain about particular writers and is always on a war-footing with one paper or another. Since the broadcasting of a documentary about the business dealings of his son, who was involved as an agent in United, he has been boycotting the BBC. In 2003 he also stopped turning up at press conferences after the final whistle. Only before and after Champions League matches does Sir Alex still grant journalists an audience – UEFA imposes harsh fines on managers who fail to talk to the press. The rare contact he has with English writers is not always amenable. Like all autocrats, Sir Alex has developed an acute persecution complex: he seems convinced that the FA, UEFA, FIFA, CIA, FBI and the rest of the world have conspired against him, and that the English press in particular are out to destroy him. To be fair to him the old Kurt Cobain adage does ring true for all Premier League managers: 'Just because you're paranoid doesn't mean they aren't after you.'

As a German, I do wonder why England's newspapers are so merciless. Agitation and a tendency to hysteria are not exactly part of this nation's disposition. The Swiss might disagree, but to this observer there really is no more polite and civilised country in the world. Tube drivers apologise for thirty-second delays; if you step on somebody's foot *they* will say sorry. Nobody answers by saying 'No' to a question; people prefer to say 'That's difficult', or 'It might not be possible', so as not to appear rude. The famous British affixes to questions – 'It is cold today, isn't it?' – are so popular because they kindly open the door for the other person, in case they have a different opinion. In England, people do not shout in the streets (when sober). But they make up for it with deafening noise on the sports pages.

Lipton explains, 'Here, newspapers have always had the job

of expressing things that people only think in secret. Take the papers from the eighteenth or nineteenth centuries – the political cartoons of the time were unbelievably aggressive. We see ourselves as warriors for the common good and the mouthpiece of the small man; we have a go at authority for him. Nobody is spared, not even the royal family. And each time we talk to a manager or a footballer we ask ourselves, "Why is this lying bastard lying to me?" '

'Relations could be more civil,' says press spokesman 'Peter Smith'. 'Personally, I think the clubs should adopt the European model of a much more open media policy. Instead of the press conferences that take place here once a week with the manager they should have them every other day with important players. Then the papers wouldn't have to go sniffing around in foreign publications for the odd suspect quote. The pressure to twist every half sentence would be less severe if there were a greater flow of information.' But Smith knows he stands no chance with these enlightened ideas. 'A very prominent manager once told me that he preferred press spokesmen who had absolutely no idea about football. Our job is to try and keep the press as far away from the team as possible, and we're expected to say "No" to every question. That's how successful media management is understood here.'

'The press spokesmen at the big clubs are very scared,' Winter confirms. 'They are scared that the coach will hold them personally responsible for a negative interview or a bad story. That's why most of them obstruct interviews. Access to the players is our biggest problem.' When the clubs became indecently rich and powerful in the nineties, arrogance set in, he says. Only television is being served now. They pay for it, after all. And these days the players are far too rich to bother giving interviews for a few thousand quid extra, unlike in the old days. 'What we can offer isn't even pocket money to them,' Lipton says.

Football writers have it much easier in Germany. At the beginning of the 1970s, when German football was at its strongest, the left-liberal idea of the responsible citizen, critical of authority, took hold in the Federal Republic. With it came the call for 'responsible patients', and 'responsible players' (*mündige Spieler*). Since clubs have to be run as democratic, transparent organisations and must be majority-owned by their members, leading officials, managers and players feel a civic duty to answer to their electorate (or customer base). Sports journalism benefits from this pressure to communicate and naturally defined it as model behaviour a long time ago. You might argue that we have taken this openness to an extreme, too, as a consequence. A German footballer *must* take a verbal stance on issues, is expected to discuss problems in public and, above all, should also be ready to criticise superiors and fellow players if he wants to be considered a truly great player, or *Führungsspieler* (leader on the pitch). Media-shy players are often dismissed as egotists or grouches lacking in character.

By contrast, it is drilled into the English professional early on that he should scream his head off during the ninety minutes then keep his mouth shut afterwards. The wagon-cart mentality invoked by many managers determines the dealings with the press. Here, clubs are companies and they do not care for employees who divulge business secrets. Even factual, mild criticism of fellow players or tactics is transformed into a corrosive attack on team spirit on the back pages, and is naturally punished with fines. Outspoken players soon gain the reputation of being divisive or trouble-makers. If a foreigner tries to play politics with the media – as he is used to doing at home – he finds himself on the bench. He has talked to the enemy, he is a traitor. Players keep all the semi-interesting stories for their autobiographies in any case; the serialisation rights alone can be worth a fortune. At the age of twenty-nine Beckham had already written three volumes of memoirs.

Unlike in Germany, interviews are not copy-approved before publication; consequently, a greater proportion of careless statements make it into the papers. 'In the Bundesliga, Jens Lehmann was used to being able to read through his interviews before they went to press. But I told him that in our country not even the Prime Minister has the right to authorise articles,' Winter says. The difference is not merely one of convention. In England, the legal copyright does not rest with the speaker but with whoever records the spoken word. In Germany, however, the player owns the copyright and can therefore remove unwanted passages before publication, or even rewrite them. I found that Lehmann was particularly dedicated to this process, to the point of changing commas.

Everything was better in the past, obviously. English pros could be induced to come out with interesting comments with a few notes; before away games, journalists and players would drink one another under the table; as late as the 1990s newspapers still benefited from the 'carousel culture' (Winter) – they flew in the same planes and chatted to the players at the luggage conveyor belt. Winter explains, 'It was Glenn Hoddle [manager 1996–99] who first banned us from the team hotel.' In spite of his relatively successful tenure – England reached the quarter-finals at the World Cup in France – the press had it in for Hoddle. When the former Spurs player revealed inside information about his team in a book after the tournament and then offended disabled people in a *Times* interview – 'You and I have been physically given two hands and two legs and half-decent brains. Some people have not been born like that for a reason. The karma is working from another lifetime' – the media cut to the chase and forced his resignation. Unfortunately, they have remained unwanted in the team hotel.

What brought this privilege to an end was an infamous boozing session. In 1996 an England squad led by Paul Gascoigne drank themselves senseless on a trip to Hong Kong. 'There was nothing about it in the sports pages because the journalists were themselves still hung-over two days later,' Winter recalls. 'It was a news reporter who broke the story.' Football writers cannot stand news reporters, since the latter make their job even more difficult. These colleagues from the news department go sniffing around for scandals and are not really interested in football as such. 'They rummage through players' dustbins, restaurant bills left on tables are pocketed. At a press conference a news reporter from the *Mail* once grabbed the microphone and asked David Beckham about his parents' divorce,' Winter says. 'You can imagine just how much he felt like discussing the following day's game with us after that.' Another favourite, if probably illegal, ploy is to ring players' mobile phones and hack the pin code to their voicemail. 'They really don't care about anything,' Lipton complains about the 'Rottweilers', as they are known in the business. 'They turn a player over and are never seen again. We have to clear up the mess afterwards.'

Not too many footballers understand that the sports writers have nothing to do with the front pages; many could not care less. Following the disclosure of his affair with Rebecca Loos, for example, Beckham tried to expel the *Sun* and *Mail* sports journalists from the England camp. All journalists showed solidarity and Beckham had to abandon the selective boycott. Rio Ferdinand, on the other hand, had no problem at all with getting paid £100,000 for writing a sports column for the *Sun*, even though the paper's front page was laying into him over women stories or his 'forgotten' drugs test. In spring 2005, Arsenal's Ashley Cole was caught by the *News of the World* negotiating illegally with Chelsea in a London hotel, and was hit with a £100,000 fine by the Football League. He recovered a large proportion of this sum a few weeks later for an exclusive interview with the same paper.

'The news reporters are the worst of all,' 'Peter Smith' says, shaking his head. 'Because they're not part of the football set-up and they know that we can't threaten them with sanctions, they are completely reckless.' For the most part they do not have to try too hard, actually. England's footballers are partial to a bit of boozy night-clubbing and the odd illicit encounter. The girls involved can hope to sell their story to one of the tabs. Lead stories in the *News of the World*, the Sunday paper from the *Sun* stable, are invariably of a sexual nature; the publication is affectionately known as 'The News of the Screws' in the business. 'Sometimes it's just a matter of who gets to the girl first, the paper or the club. A few thousand pounds and the story is dead before it's reached the light of day,' Smith says.

Minor scandals are still being published all the time. In tabloid-speak, a sex act always becomes a fiendish sex romp lasting several hours. In *Playing Away: The A–Z of Soccer Sex Scandals*, Matthew Clark assembled 220 pages of the most absurd antics of the last forty years. The spectrum ranges from Rooney's brothel visits and team baths with porn stars to dogging in car parks. In this country even a banal case of adultery can be written up as a 'scandal', and players do not even have to be stars to end up on the front page. Dramatically mediocre footballers such as Blackburn's Gary Flitcroft have also made appearances.

The combination of football, money and sex is simply irresistible material. The articles never forget to mention that the player drove his conquest back to his multi-million-pound home in a very expensive sports car. The blatant hypocrisy of the papers, which castigate footballers or other prominent individuals over their sex lives on one page and drool over a topless girl on the next, does not escape the reader. It only adds to the guilty pleasure of reading this rubbish.

'In England there is no right to privacy, even if you are barely in the public eye,' Smith says. 'And the papers will always justify their revelations by saying that footballers are role models for young people.' The social background of the players is a critical factor, of course. 'Yobs with more money than sense are seen as a legitimate target,' Rob Draper explains, 'because they openly violate the social norms. They have achieved status and fortune "too early", and their sexual misdeeds are seen as further proof of their contempt for the rules. And so they must be punished for their digression in public.'

The middle-class cricket heroes, on the other hand, can afford to be a little more indulgent. After winning the Ashes in summer 2005 Flintoff and the other England boys arrived roaring drunk at a reception with Tony Blair. Even the *Mail*, the concerned housewives' rag, hailed them as cheeky lads.

Stephen Wagg writes that at major tournaments, 'any follower of British football through the tabloids could expect, aside from the twin peaks of National Humiliation and National Rejoicing, some cocktail of Players Seen Breaking Curfew/Player Had Sex With Hotel Maid/Yob Fans on the Rampage'. Kraut-bashing is optional. 'Being anti-German is our default mode,' Lipton says, shrugging his shoulders, as if this kind of institutional resentment was an essential component of sports reporting.

Before the Euro 96 semi-final against Germany, the *Mirror* put a picture of defender Stuart Pearce in a soldier's helmet on the front page with the headline: ACHTUNG SURRENDER! FOR YOU, FRITZ, ZE WAR IS OVER. Even by British standards this silly chauvinism was excessive, bringing the paper much criticism and a reprimand from the government. And it could have been much worse. The former *Mirror* editor Piers Morgan related in his memoirs that he had chartered an old Spitfire plane to drop copies of the *Mirror* over the Germans' training ground. He called off the stunt at the last moment.

The atmosphere was so heated that after England lost the penalty shoot-out at Wembley German cars were vandalised up and down the land. In Trafalgar Square, a VW was destroyed in front of the cameras by an angry mob, even though the owners were inside at the time and shouting 'We're English!' with tears in their eyes.

Lipton believes that 'we all learned from Euro 96'. Until the next high-profile match, maybe. The Portuguese simply don't make for convincing villains.

'The press and English football are like unhappy lovers who aren't really suited to each other, but who can't separate either,' Winter says. 'Our relationship is similar to that between Richard Burton and Elizabeth Taylor: either we're head over heels in love or we're at each other's throats. There's nothing in between. But we normally kiss and make up soon enough. Then the whole thing starts again from the beginning.'

CHAPTER 8

Bungs, Backhanders and Manila Envelopes: The Dark Side of the Beautiful Game

Sex, alcohol and occasional drug-taking are the well-documented sins of English football. But what about genuine scandals, rigged matches and corruption? One might claim that the spirit of fair play prevents the most serious transgressions, but unfortunately that would not be true. In reality, the only reason we read relatively little about football's underbelly is because English media law favours the accused too much. Fearing libel action, the media disclose only a tiny fraction of the ugly stuff they know about. Or think they know about.

It took, for example, seventy years before probably the most blatant football fraud ever committed was openly discussed. At the heart of the affair was the grand old London club of Arsenal, the epitome of nobility, elegance and respectability (there were marble halls at Highbury). The Gunners are very proud of the fact that they are the only club never to have been relegated since the expansion of the First Division in 1919.

But how did they get into the top flight to begin with? In

1914–15, the last season before the war, Arsenal finished in fifth place in the Second Division. On resumption of league football in 1919 the First Division was increased in size from twenty to twenty-two teams. Everybody assumed that Derby and Preston, the winners and runners-up of Division Two, would be promoted to the First Division, and they were. The League management committee, though, had other plans for the third promotion spot. Tottenham, the bottom-placed team in Division One, were relegated to the Second Division and in Spurs' place not Barnsley, the third-placed team from Division Two, but Arsenal went up. The League has never explained this mysterious decision. 'There was no logical explanation,' David Conn writes in *The Beautiful Game? Searching for the Soul of Football.* He then proceeds to deliver one: Arsenal's owner, Sir Henry Norris, simply bribed the League manager. Simon Inglis implicitly supports this theory in the official history of the League's hundred-year existence. Even Arsenal's club biography speaks openly of 'the most audacious endeavour ever undertaken in English football' and cautiously suggests that the undeserved promotion was bought with a backhander. 'Like all the proudest aristocrats, Arsenal, when you look into it, turn out to have built their status and fortune on long-ago, best-forgotten acts of piracy,' Conn writes.

Tottenham fans have still not forgiven their neighbours for the unfair demotion. Barnsley, moreover, had to wait until 1997 before they reached the top division with their German amateur Lars Leese in goal. Their Premier League adventure was over after just one season.

The first case of match fixing took place even earlier than Arsenal's mysterious promotion. In 1905 Manchester City's captain, Billy Meredith, the 'Prince of Wingers', was caught in a bribery attempt. He had offered his Aston Villa counterpart ten pounds for a victory. When the League heard Meredith's case, it transpired that the City chairman was giving players illegal bonus payments to circumvent the upper wage limit of four pounds per week. Meredith, who always played with a toothpick in his mouth, founded the players' union two years later and fought the League for higher wages.

December 1914 saw the second match-fixing scandal. So many people had placed bets on a 2–0 victory for Manchester United against Liverpool that one bookmaker refused to pay out afterwards. Eventually a Liverpool player admitted to having thrown the game. Eight players were banned for life. After the war the punishment was overturned for seven of them because they had fought commendably. For United's Sandy Turnbull the pardon came too late: he had died at the front.

In 1965 ten players were sentenced to imprisonment for fraud, including the England player Tony Kay (Ipswich and Everton). In 1962 he had bet £50 on his side's defeat. He got £100 in return. And a life ban. 'For £100 he gave up one of the greatest football careers,' his lawyer said in court. 'He was tempted once and fell for it.' The affair also involved David 'Bronco' Layne (Sheffield United) and England player Peter Swan. Since then, no other English professional has been convicted of bribery.

It took a further thirty years before another alleged match-fixing player went before a court. Bruce Grobbelaar, the Liverpool keeper from Zimbabwe, was a clown between the posts and a true Anfield legend. In the 1984 European Cup final against Roma he unsettled the Italians so much with his comic knee trembling on the goal line that Liverpool won their fourth cup in the penalty shoot-out. (The 'spaghetti-legs' ploy came good a second time for the Reds, twenty-one years later. 'Do it like Grobbelaar!' Jamie Carragher shouted to Jerzy

Dudek before the penalties in the Champions League final in Istanbul. The Pole fidgeted wildly, the Milanese missed.)

Like most former heroes, Grobbelaar could today enjoy a cushy job in television or as an after-dinner speaker. Unfortunately he decided to accept a wad of money from a Malaysian gambler, Richard 'The Short Man' Lim, in the autumn of his career. His weakness was greed for money; his bad luck was his age. At the beginning of the nineties Grobbelaar, born 1957, witnessed people suddenly earning million-pound salaries all around him. He was only on £150,000, however, so was not averse to the idea of throwing games for similar sums. With the help of Chris Vincent, a former friend of Grobbelaar's from Zimbabwe, the *Sun* succeeded in taping a confession from the goalkeeper on film.

On 9 November 1994 the front page screamed GROBBELAAR TOOK BRIBES TO FIX GAMES. Together with Lim and Wimbledon players John Fashanu and Hans Segers, the goalkeeper was charged with conspiracy to corrupt. The jury were shown video images of players; Arsenal's goalkeeping coach, Bob Wilson, was brought in as an expert. But the footage was not conclusive. Grobbelaar alternated between brilliant saves and strange errors, with no recognisable pattern. 'I dived into the wrong bloody corner,' the goalkeeper had complained to his friend after he had actually parried a ball in a game against Manchester United. 'There's nothing you can do against your instincts. It cost me £125,000.' (Liverpool came back from 3–0 down at half-time to get a 3–3 draw against United. Alex Ferguson thought it was the best game in the history of the Premier League.)

The jury could not agree on a verdict, and the players were acquitted. In the retrial, the accused were acquitted again. Grobbelaar was off the hook. But he made the huge mistake of not quitting while ahead. Eager to extract money, he sued the

Sun for compensation for damage to his reputation. The jury found in his favour. The paper had to pay Grobbelaar £85,000 and more than a million pounds in lawyers' fees. The *Sun* appealed. After a detailed examination of all the evidence the Court of Appeal judges came to the conclusion that the jury's verdict had been 'perverse' and thus could not stand. For them Grobbelaar was 'obviously' guilty and his statements were 'literally unbelievable'. Now Grobbelaar himself appealed. The House of Lords, the highest court in the land, decided formally in his favour. In its ruling it said that the stories in the *Sun* had gone beyond the 'attempted fraud' charge laid down by the state prosecutor and had overtly accused Grobbelaar of deliberately having let in goals. This accusation had not been subsequently proven, therefore the verdict of the jury in the libel action could not have been 'perverse'. As compensation, however, Grobbelaar received the derisory sum of one pound. According to the law lords his reputation was no longer worth much more as there was no doubt about his guilt with regard to accepting bribes. 'He had acted in a way in which no decent or honest footballer would act,' declared Lord Bingham.

David Thomas summarised the verdict in his book *Foul Play*: 'Bruce Grobbelaar wanted to throw matches, he conspired to throw football matches, he accepted money to throw football matches. He just wasn't very good at actually throwing football matches.' So Grobbelaar was not only corrupt, but incompetent to boot. He was declared bankrupt. The case had ruined him financially.

Three Asian amateur electricians acted somewhat more skilfully. On 3 November 1997, a typically wet Monday evening, West Ham are playing Crystal Palace at Upton Park. The Eagles are 2–0 up at half-time in this London derby. But the Hammers hit back. Frank Lampard scores in the sixty-fifth minute to make it 2–2. Then the floodlights suddenly go out. The lighting installation is defective. The match is abandoned.

On 22 December 1997, a typically wet Monday evening, Wimbledon are playing Arsenal at Selhurst Park. The Gunners are under pressure. It is 0–0 in this London derby at half-time. One minute after the restart, the lights suddenly go out. The lighting installation is defective. The match is abandoned.

Thursday, 11 February 1999. In two days' time Charlton Athletic will be playing Liverpool on a typically wet Saturday afternoon. Chee Kew Ong, forty-nine, Eng Hwa Lim, thirty-five – both from Malaysia – and Wai Yuen Liu, thirty-seven, from Hong Kong, are arrested at the Valley Stadium; they have been caught fiddling with the floodlighting installation. The game can take place as scheduled. Charlton win 1–0.

It later emerged in court that the three defendants had inserted switches into the power sets at Upton Park and Selhurst Park that could cause a short-circuit by remote control. The Asian men were thus able to guarantee the 'right' result. In betting, if a game is abandoned in the second half the score at that point counts as the final result. English newspapers speculated that the Asian betting mafia could have earned £30 million from the two manipulated results alone. Ong Chee Kew, moreover, was a close confidant of Richard Lim, the defendant in the Grobbelaar case.

It is significant that scarcely anybody remembers these events in England. The shock passed very quickly; even the Grobbelaar affair failed to leave a lasting trace in the collective memory of English football. Maybe it was because all three players were foreigners – you'd expect nothing else from them – or the fact that the cases were fairly complex. But most importantly, memory is always a selective process, especially with regard to football.

The fact that the most recent betting scandal involving English football did not create much of a stir lay in its very nature. This time it was not about goals or floodlights, but a false identity. At the 2001 Mascot Grand National, the annual race of football mascots, the winner was Freddie the Fox, the runner for the Countryside Alliance. The organisers smelled a rat because Freddie had not turned up in fluffy mascot shoes, but running spikes. It transpired that Matt Douglas, a professional hurdler, had been under the fox's coat. Shortly before the race started so many bets had been placed on Freddie the Fox that his price had plummeted from 33-1 to 10-1. He was disqualified. Dazzler the Lion, Rushden and Diamonds, was declared the winner.

Since Grobbelaar and the Malaysians, very little has been heard about fixed games. Suspiciously little, a few insiders think. A professional gambler who makes million-pound bets in Asia on European football matches is certain that Tottenham's 6–0 victory over Oldham Athletic in the League Cup in September 2004 was a bit suspicious. 'The jump in prices was too drastic. I passed on my information to the FA, but never got a reply,' says Claude Renoir (name changed), who has also sent dossiers about strange betting patterns to the German football league and UEFA in the past. No English newspaper has yet dared to print his suspicions.

Investigative journalism has a hard time in England. Fair criticism and expressing one's opinion are permitted, but if somebody is accused of a moral or legal transgression then newspaper offices and publishing houses soon face libel action. Unlike in Germany, hardly anybody bothers with injunctions or the right to reply. Libel action is much more painful for the media due to the horrific legal costs involved, and could in the past also be a highly lucrative endeavour for the plaintiff. Famous people such as Elton John and Jeffrey

Archer have been awarded damages of several hundred thousand pounds after newspaper articles cast slurs on their reputations.

The main problem for journalists is that the burden of proof in a libel action is inverted: unlike in a normal trial, the plaintiff does not have to prove the guilt of the defendant, rather the defendant has to prove their innocence. Thus the media are immediately on the defensive; they have to convince the jury that the article in question is not libellous. What is more, even an accusation hinted at between the lines can be prosecuted. Subtlety is not enough to ensure an acquittal.

Let us assume that the *Sunny Mirror* had learned from well-informed sources that coach Jimmy Smith of City FC had received a £500,000 'thank you' in a brown envelope from an agent after a transfer deal. The *SM* can only run the story if they can prove the allegation to a jury later on. But for that, either the informants must be willing to testify in court or the paper must get hold of bank account details that substantiate the accusation. Both are highly unrealistic prospects. Jimmy Smith would have a good chance of winning his case, and before a court date had even been set the *SM* would have to shell out half a million pounds in legal costs. No more is heard of the story.

Even if there is watertight proof of the disappearance of sums of money – let us say Harry Jones's old club confirms that £500,000 of the transfer fee has 'gone missing' – the *SM* must print a formal statement denying any specific accusation: 'There is no suggestion that any party behaved unlawfully.' Precisely because there is a strong suspicion of misconduct, the paper, fearing legal action, must paradoxically make out that there has been none. As a consequence, quite a few managers and agents have been able to siphon off money in relative safety – and not just since the boom of the 1990s – even though football journalists have been well informed of these shenanigans. The odd committee has looked at the problem and come up with recommendations, some of which have even been implemented. But there is no taste for strict enforcement. The Football Association and the Premier League have always preferred to look away and not make a fuss. They do not want everybody to know that there is an odious monster living in the shadows of the telegenic Premier League. The brand needs to be protected.

Just how dirty the business can be was demonstrated by an unbelievable court case in autumn 2004. Although superstar Wayne Rooney was one of the protagonists, it was curiously under-reported in the English press. Only the broadsheets dealt with the matter; the whole thing seemed simply too nasty, even for the tabloids. In any case, David Beckham had just been accused of having an affair with his beautician. Harmless kiss-and-tell stories sell better. They translate more easily to headlines and do not throw up so many uncomfortable questions.

At the Crown Court in Warrington the charge is one of blackmail. In the dock: John Hyland, a former amateur boxer, and two of his colleagues, Chris and Anthony Bacon, are 'muscle' who pass themselves off as 'security advisers'. The trio is accused of having used intimidation and the threat of violence in spring 2003 to force Rooney's agent, Paul Stretford, to pay them around £375,000.

This ignominious story begins in autumn 2002, at a time when the sixteen-year-old Liverpudlian is delighting the Premier League with his goals. Everton, his club, are negotiating an extension to his contract with improved conditions. As a youth player Rooney is earning about £85 per week; his first professional contract in January 2003 will earn him £14,000 per week. But shortly before the negotiations with Everton begin, Rooney surprisingly switches agents. His former representative, Peter McIntosh, is fired. Paul Stretford takes over. He is an influential man in football; his firm Proactive has 270 footballers and dozens of managers on its books.

Rooney's father has taken some legal advice on the matter from solicitor Kevin Dooley. The latter, who has since died, was, shall we say, an 'interesting' character; up until his death he was under investigation for fraud. More relevant, however, is the fact that Dooley used to work for Kenny Dalglish. The former Liverpool player and successful manager was a shareholder in Proactive, and a close friend of Stretford. Rooney senior says he knew nothing of the connections between Dooley and Stretford.

Rooney's first agent, Peter McIntosh, and his confidants John Hyland and the Bacon brothers, are not going to be dismissed so easily. Everybody involved understands that Rooney is soon going to be one of the best-paid footballers in the country.

Stretford offers McIntosh around £5,000 compensation. The forty-one-year-old rejects this flatly; he wants a lot more. In November 2002 the dispute is to be settled at a meeting in a London airport hotel. McIntosh brings Hyland along for moral support; Stretford has Kenny Dalglish with him; and Dalglish, who is very well respected in public and works for the BBC as a football analyst, has Tommy Adams in tow – a notorious London gangster boss with several criminal convictions. Dalglish does not want to say why. But one can assume that Adams's presence is supposed to intimidate McIntosh and Hyland.

There is no agreement between the two sides. One month

later a second meeting takes place, at which Stretford offers Hyland 50 per cent of his future earnings for representing Rooney. Hyland rejects the offer. 'He started shouting at me,' Stretford tells the court. In June 2003, at a meeting between Hyland and Stretford, Stretford claimed that the Bacon brothers suddenly charged into the room and threaten to beat Stretford up if he does not sign over to Hyland 50 per cent of all rights to the player. In the end, Stretford agrees to pay Hyland £250,000. But shortly after the handover of the money – Stretford has delivered the tidy sum in small notes in a little suitcase – Hyland receives a visit from the police. Stretford has secretly filmed the third meeting, including the Bacons' threat of violence.

Essentially, the court case hinges on this video. When Stretford is asked by the prosecutor about the effects of the threats on his health, the forty-six-year-old bursts into tears. 'Physically and emotionally I was not in a great position,' Stretford says. He has developed arthritis and a heart defect. For the prosecution there is a clear case of blackmail.

Everybody is bracing themselves for a verdict when Hyland and the Bacons are acquitted before the end of the trial. The case breaks down due to a striking discrepancy in Stretford's witness statements. Originally the agent assured the court that he only started representing Rooney in December 2002, but from Proactive documents it emerges that he was already officially working for the brawny striker in September 2002. Stretford is no longer a credible witness for the Crown; the prosecution immediately drops the case.

In 2008, the FA found Stretford guilty of seven improper conduct charges pertaining to his work for Rooney. He was fined £300,000 and suspended for eighteen months.

Soho Square has at last woken up to the inherent conflict of interest in these cases. Stretford received £1.5 million commission for his part in Rooney's £27 million transfer from Everton to Manchester United. He also earned a share of the player's salary, which by December 2008 had risen to £90,000 per week, along with £760,000 a month for image rights. 'Any lawyer behaving like that would have been barred long ago,' Hyland's defence lawyer explained to the court.

This was not the first time Stretford's name had come up. Numerous well-known managers had shares in Proactive. John Gregory, for example, signed a remarkably large number of Proactive players during his time as Aston Villa manager. Gregory owned Proactive shares and was personally represented by Stretford.

The role of Newcastle United chairman, Freddy Shepherd, in the Rooney transfer to Manchester United is also fascinating. In August 2004 Newcastle offered around £20 million for the striker. Fleet Street was baffled. The Magpies needed a defender at the time and were not exactly awash with money. But they succeeded in forcing Manchester United's hand, who originally did not want to buy Rooney until summer 2005. Newcastle upped their offer, and United paid over £27 million. Rooney's agent profited from Newcastle's pushing up of the price, because it resulted in a higher transfer fee and commission. Shepherd fiecely denied any wrongdoing and no action was taken against the club.

In 1999, the FA hired Graham Bean, a former policeman, as compliance officer, with a remit to investigate potential irregularities within the game generally. In 2003, he gave up, disillusioned. His salary had been insultingly low, and in spite of a number of promising inquiries he was never given enough support. After his resignation he had to sign an agreement that he would not talk to the press. The police are not much interested either. They have enough problems as it is.

Manchester United's chief executive, David Gill, defended

Stretford's exorbitant commission at the time. He said, 'You can't expect an eighteen-year-old to negotiate his own multi-million-pound contract. Rooney's talent is quite clearly in his feet.' In other words, the players are too daft, there is no other way. And while the football-interested public in the kingdom of kick-backs continue to let themselves be strung along and pay the highest ticket prices in the world, oblivious to the fact that millions are vanishing into the pockets of agents and managers as commissions and bungs, nothing will change. After all, everything is going just nicely.

It certainly was for Kevin Keegan, too. Although Europe's Footballer of the Year in 1978 and 1979 proved to be completely out of his depth as England manager – during the 1–0 defeat against Germany on 7 October 2000, the last game at the old Wembley Stadium and also Keegan's last as coach, he realised at half-time that he lacked the tactical knowledge to implement the necessary adjustments and later resigned in the toilet – as a Premier League manager (Fulham and Manchester City) he concluded all sorts of successful transfers. Successful transfers for Proactive, to be more precise. Like Sir Bobby Robson (Newcastle), Peter Reid (Sunderland, Leeds) and Sam Allardyce (Bolton), from 2001 the former Hamburg striker accepted Stretford's invitation to purchase Proactive shares. Later, he bought a sizeable number of players contracted to Stretford.

A court case in Denmark in July 2005 offered a striking insight into the business practices of the player agencies. On 15 May 2002 Manchester City signed the twenty-year-old Danish defender Mikkel Bischoff from AB Copenhagen on the wishes of coach Kevin Keegan. The transfer fee for this young talent was £750,000; his agent was Karsten Aabrink from Proactive Scandinavia, a daughter company of Proactive. City, the player and Copenhagen were all happy with the deal, until a year later an internal memo from Proactive Scandinavia found its way to the Copenhagen board. The memo stated that Proactive had received a payment of £350,000 from Manchester City – for a transfer that had brought Copenhagen £750,000. Board member Laust Joen Jacobsen was shocked: 'You feel as if things were rigged. A commission representing forty-seven per cent of the total sum exceeds all reasonable amounts.' FIFA's non-binding guidelines recommend 5–10 per cent commission for the agent involved – Proactive claimed that the £300,000 represents 5–10 per cent of the player's wages on his five-year contract. In the deal, moreover, there was concern that Proactive may have violated the statutes. FIFA expressly forbids agents from representing more than one party at a time. In the case of Bischoff, Proactive may have worked for both the player and Manchester City although this was never proved, and it has to be assumed that there was no impropriety in this regard. Bischoff's agent, Karsten Aabrink of Proactive Scandinavia, told the court that he had been unaware that City had asked Proactive's UK branch to arrange the move.

Afterwards, Olav Skaaning Andersen wrote in the Danish paper *Ekstra Bladet*, 'British managers have been caught receiving multi-millions in kickbacks before. The suspicion that Keegan has personally received money for the Bischoff deal is well founded . . .' Keegan, Aabrink and Proactive brought a libel action against Andersen and Palle Sorensen, the chairman of the Danish players' union, who had also spoken of a 'crooked business'. In July 2005 the Danish court found in favour of the defendants: according to Danish law their statements did not constitute libel although whether the court actually proved Keegan personally made substantial sums from the deal, or that Proactive breached FIFA rules, is unclear. Keegan and Proactive have always denied any impropriety. FIFA were investigating the matter, without result. During his three years in England Bischoff played once for Manchester City and eleven times for Wolverhampton Wanderers, who had him on loan. In March 2005 Keegan resigned.

Two years prior to that, a journalist asked him about his Proactive shares while City were on a training camp in Denmark. 'Mighty Mouse' turned red and stormed on to the team bus. In his hand he still had the half-signed shoe of a young fan.

Everybody knows the 'British managers' Andersen was referring to in his article. He chiefly meant George Graham. The former Arsenal boss is the only Premier League manager to date who has publicly admitted taking money from agents. Graham still maintains that these kick-backs in no way amounted to bribery; they were 'gifts'. An interesting interpretation, you have to give him that.

The affair got under way after the signing of the Danish midfielder John Jensen – goal-scorer in the final of the European Championship against Germany – from FC Bröndby in July 1992. After a tip-off from the Norwegian finance ministry, who were investigating the agent involved in the deal, Rune Hauge, the British tax authorities approached Graham in August 1994. The successful manager had difficulty in explaining the provenance of £425,000 in accounts he held in Ireland and Guernsey. He asked Arsenal for help. David Dein and Peter Hill-Wood, the most important board members, were astonished but didn't react at first. In Denmark, meanwhile, Henrik Madsen substantiated the accusations against Hauge and Graham in a book (*The Men from Bröndby*).

As the luck of the draw would have it, Arsenal met Bröndby in the Cup Winners' Cup in October 1994. Dein asked the board of the Danish club whether the transfer fee of around £1.5 million had been received in full. Only around £800,000 had actually arrived, the Danes answered. It transpired that the remaining £700,000 had been diverted to an account belonging to Hauge. Shortly afterwards, Hauge had paid £285,000 into Graham's account. 'It was an unsolicited gift,' Graham told the Arsenal bosses.

To avoid any damage to Arsenal's image, and as a thank you for Graham's successful work, it was decided that at the end of the season in May 1995 'they would part company by mutual consent'. But the scandal could not be kept secret for long. When the *Mail on Sunday* uncovered a second questionable transfer in December – in 1991 Graham had bought the Norwegian Pal Lydersen (IK Start) for £500,000, although he had been available for £215,000, and afterwards received £140,000 in used fifty-pound notes from Rune Hauge in a London hotel – Arsenal had to sack him.

The FA, shocked out of their lethargy, set up a commission to investigate. A lenient sentence was passed: a one-year ban and a £50,000 fine for Graham. In the opinion of the FA's lawyers the manager was only guilty of accepting money illegally, but not of bribery. The *Sun* paid £250,000 for the serial rights to his autobiography. In summer 1996 Graham was back under contract at Leeds United; these days, he works as a pundit on television. Hauge was given a lifelong ban by FIFA; after an appeal the sentence was reduced to two years.

'Arsenal's directors considered Graham's dishonesty as a football matter,' Tom Bower writes in his book *Broken Dreams: Vanity, Greed and the Souring of British Football*, 'and the football community sought to keep everything within the family. The etiquette of the business . . . was not to wash the dirty linen in public.' The affair, which Bower has researched meticulously, is not only symptomatic of the widespread 'You scratch my back . . .' culture of agents, managers and some club officials, but also of the way in which the problem has been largely ignored in England. Bungs, backhanders and brown envelopes have always been regarded as minor offences.

Shortly after Graham received his ban, Gary Lineker defended him in his *Telegraph* column. Lineker said Graham was 'a very likeable and successful man who was the scapegoat for every manager who's ever had a backhander'. Lineker's apology for Graham betrayed the extent of the practice. 'The bung, it seems, has long been commonplace . . . It was almost considered to be an acceptable perk for men who are treated so shabbily by their employers. The majority of players are, I am sure, not partial to the odd paper bag.' The legendary Bobby Charlton, interviewed by the Graham inquiry, shared this sympathetic point of view. 'Managers get abused; they'll be unfairly dismissed. So they'll take while they have the chance,' he said.

Harry Redknapp, always good for a quote, would probably endorse this theory. 'Any Premier League manager who is not a millionaire after three years has done something wrong,' said the Londoner without false modesty. In the media, Redknapp is admired as a clever wheeler-dealer, a deal-maker who is tirelessly hunting around the world for bargains for his clubs. Over the past few years questions have been asked about potential conflicts of interests; his formidable business sense is beyond dispute, however.

In 1992 eleven foreigners were playing in the top English division; in 1999 there were more than 200; in 2002 more than 400. At times one felt that all of them were signed to Redknapp's West Ham. In his seven years in charge at Upton Park he transferred no fewer than 134 players in and out. Among his acquisitions were a few stars – Paolo Di Canio, Ian Wright and Marc-Vivien Foe – as well as half an army of flops and failures. In this period alone around £130 million changed hands. But in spite of some desperate record sales (Frank Lampard for £11 million to Chelsea, Rio Ferdinand for £18 million to Leeds United) the famous East End club was on the verge of bankruptcy when his tenure came to an end in 2001.

The Rio Ferdinand transfer demonstrated that all sorts of people cashed in on Harry's countless deals. Pini Zahavi, the Israeli agent and confidant of Roman Abramovich, earned £1 million commission as Ferdinand's agent. In addition the Leeds chairman, Peter Ridsdale, authorised the payment of £1.75 million to Rune Hauge, the discredited intermediary, without consulting his board. The reason why has never been properly explained. No contractual agreement between Leeds and the Norwegian existed; Hauge had just made a few telephone calls. Ridsdale explained later that the agent had had to pay 'other people'. Meanwhile, West Ham gave Harry Redknapp £300,000 for his role in the transfer. The payment was all above board, if somewhat unusual. It was a gift from his chairman, Redknapp said, rewarding him for his management of the club.

Of course, these unsavoury things do not only occur in England. It is an open secret that the reason why so many foreigners are playing in the major European leagues is not only to do with their outrageous talents. The simple fact of the matter is that in international deals it is much easier for a few pounds/dollars/euros to be siphoned off for those involved. 'Fans are better off not knowing about all the dodgy things that go on behind the scenes,' said Klaus Toppmöller, the ex-Leverkusen manager.

Yet a very specific combination of factors has made England into 'the most corrupt football country of all', in the opinion of an Italian agent who has been involved in many big transfers. As with almost everything in England and its football, tradition plays a major part. More than a century ago hidden payments were everyday practice. It began with payments for amateurs, and continued with illegal bonuses for wins and paper bags to circumvent the upper wage limit. The unrealistic constraints achieved the very opposite of what they wanted: football did not become a noble game but a very shady business. A system developed in which semi-criminal goings-on were encouraged, if not essential to the game's survival. This specific 'business culture' has survived throughout the decades.

This is not to say that another way did not (and does not) exist. Matt Busby, the manager of the Manchester United team involved in the Munich air disaster of 1958, and a devout Catholic, was strictly opposed to hidden payments. To compensate his players he arranged a raft of perks for them: free cinema entry, golf club membership, nights at the best hotel in Blackpool. But he was the shining exception in the shadowy world of football deals in Britain.

With the influx of huge sums of money in the 1990s, dubious practices gathered pace. Multi-million-pound revenues from television contracts plunged clubs that had become wealthy almost overnight into uncontrolled buying frenzies. Like any other nouveau riche, the clubs bought up everything that shone like gold and had a big exotic name. In 1999, at the high point of the boom, around £150 million was spent on new players in a single summer. Even modest clubs like Wimbledon felt obliged to shell out £7.5 million for the lumbering Welsh striker John Hartson. Not even the most cautious club owner could escape this crazed hunt for expensive acquisitions.

Graeme Souness took matters to the extreme. In 1996 the Southampton coach got a call from a man claiming to be AC Milan's star striker, George Weah. Was Souness interested in Weah's cousin? Ali Dia, thirty, was a Senegalese national player with experience at Paris St Germain and Bologna, the man said. He was without a club, available for free. His curiosity aroused, Souness offered Dia a one-month trial contract, and brought him on in the thirty-second minute of the home game against Leeds United on 23 November. Fifty-five painful minutes later, Dia was substituted. It was quite evident that the man was no footballer, and he was not Weah's cousin either. His contract was terminated. Dia played a few times after that, for non-league Gateshead. Then he disappeared.

In Germany we say *Gelegenheit macht Diebe* – opportunity makes thieves. And the opportunity is particularly big in England. Most clubs lack the necessary control mechanisms. The basic structures have not changed for almost a hundred years. Traditionally the manager is also the general manager – an autocrat with an incredible amount of power. Above him are only the board members or chairmen. Their supervision is frequently limited to a 'yes' or 'no' regarding a desired transfer. Negotiations with players, agents and other clubs are carried out by the man on the bench. During his eight years at Highbury, George Graham bought players for a total of about £36 million. Scarcely one of his transfers was scrutinised closely by the club. And why would they have been? The Scot led Arsenal to two championships, three cup wins, and a victory in the Cup Winners' Cup.

To an extent, the FA are comfortable with their own impotence. Any harmless criticism of a referee's decision or alleged discrimination is pursued inquisitorially; the accusation is one of 'bringing the game into disrepute'. But doing things for the sake of looking busy cannot hide the fact that bigger problems are being ignored.

A third point to note, besides the immense sums of money that would tempt even the most principled of men, and the poor monitoring of these practices, is the psychological framework that managers employ to justify their greed to themselves and the fans. Some coaches imply that they do not feel so bound by honour or loyalty – held up elsewhere as important values – because as employees of the clubs they cannot expect loyalty themselves. 'At the end of the day, no one gives a monkey's about you when your career's over, so in my view you should make the bucks while you can,' Harry Redknapp said, for example.

The greedy scammer is thus transformed into an anti-establishment wide boy who gets one over 'those big shots at the top'. This charade works because British managers are exclusively ex-professionals who, just like the majority of fans, come from a working-class background and can credibly present themselves as small men engaged in a struggle for survival with their rich bosses. In England, along with the strong emphasis on playing by the rules, one finds a more secret but nevertheless widespread admiration for artful dodgers who, like the character from Dickens's *Oliver Twist*, never get caught. Lovable rogues they are, modern-day Robin Hoods, without the social redistribution bit. With clubs having broken away from their working-class roots in the course of modernisation and fans feeling alienated by organisations that have now become big firms and public companies, managers susceptible to under-the-table payments do not run a huge risk of being seen as thieves by the supporters. Backhanders for transfers have become something akin to tax evasion or insurance fraud: a petty crime that supposedly does nobody any harm.

It is the agents who are now the target. Given that the press, for the reasons cited above, have exposed so few corrupt managers, and the FA have also kept quiet, the agents have become lightning rods. The collective unease about the unchecked flow of millions is focused on them. Agent-bashing is a popular tabloid sport, though papers and pundits are not selective in their criticism and will never name names. No matter. We'll get the right ones sooner or later, they tell themselves.

The most popular accusation is repeated so often that it has now become a football truism: agents are taking too much 'money out of the game'. In July 2005, for example, under the headline £8M AGENT SHOCK, the *Evening Standard* ran an article on commissions paid to agents in the three divisions below the Premier League. 'Too much money is leaving football through payments to agents,' the paper quoted Brian Mawhinney, the Football League chairman, as saying. The idea is that football is some sort of closed loop, a zero-sum game from which agents are diverting too much into their own pockets.

The analogy is easy to understand, but does not bear up to close scrutiny. Dividends to shareholders, interest payments to banks, chairmen's salaries and players' wages do not flow back into football either. Much of this money fills swimming pools in tasteless villas which at some point will feature on MTV's *Footballers' Cribs*. Presented by Nancy Dell'Olio.

The football agent is cast as a useful bogeyman in other respects, too. If a player, say Steven Gerrard, flirts a little too closely with another club, the disappointed fan can readily blame the insidious agent. The player's open lack of loyalty is edited out. If said player does in the end renew his contract, it is easier to forgive the whole affair – after all, he was led astray by his wily agent and did not know any better.

It is impossible to gauge whether the manila envelope will eventually go the way of other English idiosyncrasies, such as group piss-ups in the training camp or the hearty steak before kick-off, and disappear. Attempts to install general managers or sporting directors alongside the coach, men who will concentrate on the business aspects of the job and prevent conflicts of interests arising, have met resistance. Stricter regulations from the Home Office that only allow a British work permit to foreign players who represent their national side are at least keeping the number of non-EU transfers down, and tougher laws on money-laundering introduced in the wake of the 11 September 2001 terrorist attacks have made it much more difficult to bank black money unnoticed. The ever-more important sponsors, moreover, have a vested interest in ensuring that their brands are not compromised.

One is left feeling less optimistic, however, by the fact that the current trend is away from public companies and back to privatised clubs. As a public company, Manchester United had to file regular accounts of income and expenditure; payments to agents were made transparent. Their new owners Glazer brothers, by contrast, can do whatever they like. The same is true of Chelsea. Fans will never find out how much commission Roman Abramovich has handed over to agents. But in his specific case it probably would not make too much difference anyway.

Sir Bobby Robson confided to the *Sunday Times* that only a minority of managers turned down bribes; he himself was once apparently offered £500,000 for a deal. In 2006, Luton Town manager Mike Newell also dared to speak out. 'A lot of people involved with the agents and doing the deals are taking backhanders,' he claimed. He said he was also offered 'a sweetener' by a club director to buy one of his players. An FA inquiry came to nothing and Newell was ostracised for his whistle-blowing; he spent two years out of a job.

At the same time, the BBC's *Panorama* was investigating corruption in football. Secretly recorded footage showed agents talking about the bribe culture, but no hard evidence was presented. The FA launched another inquiry headed by the former Metropolitan Police chief Lord Stevens. He looked at 320 transfers, a few clubs were raided, but once again no charges were brought.

We will probably only discover who has been on the take

when many of the Premier League managers are no longer with us. According to English law, the dead cannot have their reputations ruined. Libel actions from beyond the grave are not permissible.

In September 2004, shortly after the death of Brian Clough, the legendary coach, alcoholic, big mouth and European Cup winner with Nottingham Forest (1979 and 1980), Graham Bean wrote in the *Guardian*, 'There is no question bungs were paid then [in Clough's time] . . . I think the whole football world and football public just accepted that it happened and they turned a blind eye.' You can also put it differently: 'Cloughie likes a bung.' This quote comes from former England and Spurs manager Terry Venables. Clough had demanded a £500,000 backhander for the transfer of Teddy Sheringham to Spurs. Tottenham chairman Alan Sugar did not want to go along with that, yet in August 1992 Clough's assistant, Ronnie Fenton, received the sum at a motorway service station from Frank McLintock (ex-Arsenal), whom Venables had engaged as a middle man. The subsequent investigation by the Football Association lasted four years; in spite of overwhelming evidence its report reached no conclusive verdict. By that time Brian 'Old Big 'ead' Clough was already out of the firing line due to health problems.

Foul Play, *Broken Dreams*, *The Beautiful Game? Searching for the Soul of Football* – these rather dramatic titles of the few books that have dealt with the unpleasant aspects of football betray the fact that even the cynical journalists are closet romantics. Like all football fans they want to believe in fair play, and in the idea that football has a soul. They are not dreamers, but idealists.

The danger of such ideals is that you can all too easily hide behind them. When Newcastle lost 2–1 to Deportivo La Coruña in the UI Cup in July 2005, Graeme Souness complained afterwards that the Spaniards had demanded yellow cards whenever Newcastle committed a foul. 'You don't do that, it's not British,' Souness said. The goal for his side had been scored by Lee Bowyer, an ex-Leeds player who was found guilty of affray for racially abusing an Asian waiter.

CHAPTER 9

Back to the Future

A Wednesday evening, somewhere in the north of England. It is drizzling slightly, wind is whistling through the narrow lanes. Dozens of men with pale faces and red scarves are dragging young boys behind them towards a blazing light. It is about to start. Fog is pressing down on the corrugated iron roof of the small stadium. Maybe it is the smoke from the hotdog stands, in front of which young lads queue with cups of beer in their hands. It smells of grease, horse shit and hamburgers of uncertain consistency. Everything is peaceful, but the air is heavy with tension and adventure. You might want to eat one of these burgers to impress your mates, it would show some mettle. You drink, you sing, you wear your team's colours with pride. This is how it should be. This is football in England. In the cinema.

'This one's for the fans' is the name of the Coca-Cola ad campaign, and the accompanying song is so catchy that by the end of the advert some in the cinema audience are happily mumbling along. British advertising is the best in the world; it has an infallible lock on moods and trends. 'For the fans' hits the nail on the head. The clip evokes an idyll, the yearning for a past when football was a touch smaller, more intimate, more emotional and above all more authentic. For once, it is not melancholy that drips from the screen but hope. Look here, the advert says, it can be different. Let us go back to our roots. Away from commercialism, from club mega-stores, and from players who earn £150,000 per week and kiss the badge while secretly mulling over a transfer. We can make it happen together. We can get our football back.

Every fantasy is the flipside to the problems of reality. At present there is plenty to worry about. Average attendance figures in the Premier League have been flat-lining around the 36,000 mark for five years (the Bundesliga had 41,000 in 2008–09). The overbearing dominance of the Big Four dampens enthusiasm. Kick-off times dictated by television make it sometimes impossible for away fans to go to watch their team. In any case, you do not actually have to go to the ground any more. At the turn of the century, one measly game could be seen live, on Sunday, and you had to wait until half past ten on a Saturday night to see a round-up of the games. Sky and Setanta now broadcast up to five live matches every weekend, and extended highlights are available on Saturday evenings.

Everything evolves around money. Since the establishment of the Premier League in 1992, ticket prices have been increasing faster than the average wage. New customers from the middle classes discovered the violence-free, entertaining football of the nineties and fuelled the boom. But now prices have reached a hazardous level. The cheapest regular Premier League ticket for an adult in the 2008–09 season was £15 (Aston Villa). Anybody wanting to see Arsenal had to pay at least double that amount. Plenty of English fans have started travelling to Europe at weekends; a game at Dortmund can set you back as little as ten euros. You can drink beer and stand on the terraces, too.

Fulham, West Ham and Chelsea have been placing adverts in the *Evening Standard* before home games, informing readers of the availability of large numbers of tickets. A real novelty. And in Manchester it was rumoured that the club had to give away thousands of tickets secretly to schools, in order to fill Old Trafford in the wake of the Glazer backlash. This was before the new quadrants increased stadium capacity to 75,000 seats.

'The game ate itself,' wrote the *Observer* in 2005. The atmosphere inside the grounds has certainly changed. The rise in ticket prices has radically altered the demographic inside the stadiums. In 1997 only 19 per cent of Premier League fans earned more than £30,000 per year; in 2000 this figure had reached 33 per cent. Arsenal's Highbury, where the spectators were more affluent than average, was sarcastically called 'the library' by other fans, and the main stand was known as the 'accountants' stand'. Incredibly, the new Emirates Stadium is even quieter. It is not much different at Stamford Bridge. In spite of the ground's relatively small capacity of 43,000, group-stage Champions League matches are frequently not sold out, and the atmosphere can be decidedly lukewarm. But who is supposed to be making the noise if the grass-roots fans are squeezed out? The well-heeled customers increasingly have the game to their own and wonder why the ground is so quiet. In November 2000 Manchester United's captain Roy Keane was moved to rant about the 'prawn sandwich' brigade in the expensive seats who had no idea about football, and who did not give the team proper support.

Nonetheless, going to a football match in England continues to be a unique experience, prawns or no prawns, especially when local rivals or top teams meet. Is there another country in the world where a relegated team which has just been thrashed in the decisive match will be given a standing ovation by sobbing fans? (This happened on the last day of the 2004–05 season, when Norwich lost 6–0 to Fulham.)

Yet one cannot dismiss the view that it used to be much more thrilling, louder and more exciting as simply nostalgic claptrap. Some fan representatives have started to call for a return to terraces. 'I have to laugh when managers complain about the lack of atmosphere in the stadium,' says Colin Hendrie of the Independent Manchester United Supporters Association (IMUSA). 'The truth is that clubs in fact do all they can to prevent a good atmosphere. Since ticket sales are done electronically and you're normally only allowed to buy two tickets per person, I have to sit next to strangers in the stadium. Also, the stewards are much too strict. If you stand up for a few minutes, someone immediately comes along and gives you a warning. "Sit back down or you'll be out." '

The zero-tolerance policy on violence and racist utterances, extremely commendable measures that the rest of the world looked up to, as well as a general ban on smoking (there are very strict constraints on the selling of alcohol, too) made nineties football into an entertainment product for all social classes. The Premier League were, in all likelihood, not exclusively guided by altruistic motive. In any case, they recognised that the established marginalisation of entire population groups in the grounds was bad for business. Scenes such as the one during Bayern Munich's 2–0 victory over Besiktas (September 1997), when the home fans held up scores of Aldi plastic bags in Munich's Olympic Stadium to mock their opponents' shopping habits, were and are completely unimaginable in England. It has been a long time since phrases along the lines of 'We don't want Spaniards/Dutch/English pigs', a common occurrence at European matches in Bundesliga stadiums, have been heard in English grounds.

There are, however, borderline cases that are difficult to resolve in the age of political correctness. Gabriele Marcotti, an Italian football journalist in London, remembers the time when a steward moved to evict his friend from the stadium during an Arsenal–Chelsea game. Each time a certain member of the Gunners side touched the ball, Marcotti's friend had made monkey noises. 'We don't tolerate racism here,' the steward griped, grabbing the offender by the collar. The man protested his innocence, explaining that his noises had been aimed at Gunners defender Martin Keown. To be sure, the centre-back's broad nose, fuzzy hair, very big eyes and ungainly movements did bear some superficial resemblance to a primate from human evolutionary history. The steward heard who was being insulted, thought about it for a moment, and then let Marcotti's friend go again. 'Oh I see,' he said. 'That's all right then.' Because Keown is, of course, a white man.

Homophobic slogans and chants will be the next to be banned. Again, that is to be applauded. Yet there is fear spreading among supporters that the authorities are going too far in their push towards making the game family friendly, and there is indeed a worry that grounds are becoming sterile, ethically cleansed zones. If the space around the green rectangle is to be subject to the draconian laws of Singapore, and each minute act of anti-social behaviour (spitting, chewing gum, making the 'wanker' gesture) or insult is to be prohibited, surely a key element of football's social function will be lost: football furnishes an Englishman with the opportunity to break the social code of conduct in a controlled way. For ninety minutes, the normal laws of human coexistence that are particularly adhered to in England can be safely ignored. The crudest insults, the worst swear words, the nastiest jokes . . . in England these are either heard outside pubs and clubs in the small hours, or in the stadium. Nowhere else.

'The whole ghastly secret, vile, dark laundry basket of young Englishmen's fears, prejudices and braggadocio is tipped out under the floodlights and bellowed at the top of their voices,' A. A. Gill writes in his book *The Angry Island*. 'It's hideous and invigorating and group therapy, and it's like watching a sitcom where the studio audience has all the best lines.'

Football does not only allow people to articulate feelings of hatred, however. It also allows for a kind of sentimentality that is frowned upon in everyday life; it acts as a safety valve for the soul of a buttoned-up nation. If you hear a man talking proudly about love in the street, on the train, at the post office or at a dinner party, you can be certain he is not referring to his wife or girlfriend, but his football club. 'The love for one's club is the first and everlasting love of a young man,' the *Guardian* wrote. In Italy, Mamma comes first, then the ball.

Talking of Mamma: more than half of all Premier League fans give 'family tradition' as the reason for supporting their club. Most men first went to the ground with their father. The game brings English fathers and sons together, in a magical kind of way that does not require either of them to say very much. Years later, fans associate going to the ground with feelings of warmth and security they might have stopped experiencing as an adult. In English society, being close to one's family is not that important. On the whole relatives are more often seen as an embarrassment or a burden. When Christmas approaches, the newspapers are full of practical tips about how to survive the ghastly days with one's family – without the copious consumption of several litres of alcohol.

The proverbial aloofness of English people is probably not a psychological phenomenon per se, rather a matter of convention and politeness: men consciously avoid talking about their feelings because it might make the other person feel quite uncomfortable and turn him into an involuntary intruder into somebody's private business. Feelings are best not brought out into the open too much. The kind of TV chat shows where cuckolded husbands are reconciled with their wives, or adopted children are reunited with their biological mothers, are different from their US or German counterparts. They don't seem to be geared towards forcing great emotional outpourings – the English prefer not to see things like that. Jeremy Kyle and others would rather admonish their predominantly working-class guests for their irresponsible behaviour until they agree to change their ways.

The quite unbelievable outbreak of public mourning following the death of Princess Diana in August 1997 could only have come as a result of media brainwashing, Jeremy Paxman was convinced. 'Diana's funeral had brought forth scenes of public mourning so bizarrely "un-English" – the lighting of candles in the park, the throwing of flowers on to her passing coffin – that the wartime generation could only look on as baffled travellers in their own land. The flower-throwers had learned their behaviour from watching television, for it is a Latin custom: the potency of the mass media can hardly be exaggerated.'

So television is to blame if the stiff upper lip starts to tremble. Or, perhaps, a lack of temperament. In October 2004, in the aftermath of the murder of engineer Ken Bigley in Iraq, Boris Johnson criticised Liverpudlians for being addicted to grief. The inhabitants of the city were 'wallowing' in their 'victim status', Johnson wrote in the *Spectator*, adding that this was part of their 'deeply unattractive psyche'. In the same article the politician also expressed his view that criticism of the police after the 1989 Hillsborough catastrophe, in which ninety-six Liverpool fans died, had been exaggerated. He was forced by his party to take a trip to Merseyside in order to apologise. (A year or so later, Johnson could chortle at the news that dozens of Scousers had placed flowers and cards of condolence by an alley where a strangely deformed foetus had been found. 'Rest in peace, little baby,' one card said, 'safe in Jesus' arms. From a loving mother.' The police quickly found out that the mysterious baby was actually a dead chicken.)

But back to love. An Englishman may contemplate cheating on his wife or switch from Tories to Labour after twenty years, but he will never – NEVER! – forsake his football club. Fans are not quite so unconditional in their support vis-à-vis the players themselves, but they are, by continental standards, terribly indulgent.

A player who gives the impression that he would die for the club's colours can get away with anything, even with public demands for more money. In 2000, when Roy Keane spent months haggling over a higher salary, he had the supporters on his side. They felt he had earned his millions with his loyal service. When he finally signed – he was a whisker away from moving to Bayern Munich on a free transfer– the United fans were not envious of the star's riches, but proud – proud that the best midfield player in the league at that time was playing for their club. In England they would never sing *Scheiss Millionäre* (millionaire bastards) at their own players, the way they often do in the Bundesliga.

'In Germany you have to think quite carefully about which car you use to come to training, because there might be negative reactions,' Dietmar Hamann explains. 'In Liverpool there is a lot of poverty, but the attitude is completely different. Men come along with their sons, point at the players' cars and say, "Look here, son! If you make an effort and work hard, you'll be able to afford something like that one day."'

The holy marriage between fan and club is the last rock-solid monogamous relationship in the Western world. Even the most obsessed follower of a pop group will not confine himself to buying their, and only their, records. Clubs, on the other hand, have their customers exclusively, and for life. With so much unconditional love, one party is sadly easily tempted to benefit materially. Long before the Glazers' takeover Manchester United were the undisputed masters of transforming affection into hard cash. The record title-holders of the Premier League used to bring out up to four different shirts per season, in the full knowledge that the supporters could not resist. The same mechanism brought about the continual rise in ticket prices. But recently clubs have been a little too blatant in their hunt for new, wealthier suitors. The fans have belatedly recognised that their loyalty is one-sided. They will no longer tolerate a lover who is only interested in material things at any price.

'Football is at a crossroads,' says Phil French, the chairman of Supporters Direct. His lobby group, financed by the government, has been representing supporters' concerns since 2000, and has never enjoyed as much influence or popularity. 'Football is at a crossroads,' Premier League chief executive Richard Scudamore agrees. 'After ten years of continual growth we're now seeing the first losses,' French says. 'It's a classic case: an industry has boomed for so long that it doesn't think it has to look after the fans, or – I hate to say it – customers any more. Now they're paying the price.' The recession is likely to strengthen this sense of disenchantment.

Concern about the numbers going to the grounds is attracting the most attention because empty seats do more than damage to the brand. In spite of a television contract worth £900 million a year, ticket sales still constitute the single largest source of income for most clubs. But there is much more to this. Many supporters seem to have become tired with being cast as consumers, and want to reconquer football for themselves. There is widespread talk of the struggle for 'the game's soul'. In less dramatic terms, it is a fight about power and participative management.

The problem is as old as English football itself. In 1892, a century before the first German clubs were transformed into limited and public companies, the English clubs were already run as firms. Professionalism brought in its wake an end to democratic structures. In order to be able to pay the players the clubs needed to attract rich businessmen as investors; founding a company was the simplest method of raising capital. Around the turn of the century every professional club was in private hands.

The owners knew that they could count on material support from the fans. They helped to set up supporters' clubs and employed the members – without pay – as ground stewards and programme sellers. Whenever a club lacked money, the bosses would appeal to the common good and ask the supporters' clubs for donations. These organised lotteries collected thousands of pounds per year. In return they got . . . nothing. For a hundred years there was not a single fan representative on the board of a professional club. Whenever the supporters demanded a say in club affairs there was no more talk of the community. The owners dismissed them, pointing to the business structure. The demand for transparency of, and access to, club finances was also rejected. 'I am sure the supporters of the Club would appreciate it very much if the directors would take them into their confidence and publish the "gates" for every match and the amounts of transfers for players,' a Leicester Fosse (later Leicester City) fan wrote to the *Leicester Mercury* in 1913. Ten years later another reader's letter in the newspaper advocated the appointment of two supporters to the board. The line of argument can be found in any fanzine today: 'The Club is, properly speaking, an institution of the town, and not a kind of private trading company, conducted at the whim of the few men who are at the moment immediately interested.'

After the Second World War the clubs treated their fans even more shabbily, falling attendances notwithstanding. The new Sky Blue stand at Coventry's Highfield Road ground was financed in 1964 exclusively by supporters – for more than £27,000. In addition, they took on the club's £40,000 debt to the banks (worth around £400,000 in today's money). The chairman of the board, Jimmy Hill, refused to give the fans a guarantee that they would be allowed to use the new facilities built with their own money.

The Ipswich Town supporters' association modernised the Portman Road ground with their own funds after the war; between 1957 and 1965 the members raised £90,000. How did the club display its gratitude? It dissolved the fan club by decree in 1967 and replaced it with a new supporters' club under direct control of the firm's board.

In 1971 sociology professor Ian Taylor explained the hooligan phenomenon, still new at the time, as the result of the alienation supporters felt at their club's changed values. The 'gentrification' and commercialisation of the sport had placed them in opposition to the players and the authorities. The main point of his 'speculative sociology of football' was the thesis that the supporters had lost 'the illusion of participative control' over the fate of their club, and had reacted to this with a different, more direct form of participation. They stormed pitches or violently defended their territory, which for the most part was a stand behind the goal.

Post-Hillsborough changes in legislation have made this sort of imagined resistance impossible today. The feelings of alienation, impotence and dependence have remained, however. Rogan Taylor's conclusion from 1991 is still relevant eighteen years later: unburdened by supporter control, the respected academic wrote, 'clubs and the game's authorities generally repeatedly cashed in on the indefinable – hence "religious" almost – enthusiasm that supporters showed for the game'.

Football clubs are monopolists. The combination of guaranteed cash-flow, strong emotions and instantaneous celebrity status is irresistible to tycoons and wannabes. Moreover, the extremely lax regulations that govern the buying and selling of private companies here make entry into this business far less complicated than in other countries. (Prior to his takeover of Chelsea, Roman Abramovich had cast an eye over Real Madrid and Barcelona, but quickly realised that because of their democratic structures – the clubs belong to the members – it was impossible to buy them.)

English football has become a subsection of the City, London's banking district. It attracts foreign capital like a light attracts moths. The most obvious reason why the Premier League has managed to outspend La Liga and Serie A has to do with an unbelievably favourable tax regime and unregulated streams of money flowing into the game from all corners of the world. England, the country of tradition, is the place where globalisation has left its strongest mark. Nationality is but an afterthought.

It is only to be expected that foreign masters, lacking any natural association with the town or the club's history, should arouse great suspicion. But you do not need chancers and inept owners from abroad to ruin a club, the English are quite capable of doing that themselves. Following their insanely wasteful transfer policy and the construction of Chelsea Village, a naff hotel and restaurant complex around the stadium, Ken Bates's Chelsea, with more than £80 million worth of debt, were on the verge of bankruptcy before Abramovich bailed them out. At Leeds, Peter Ridsdale's profligate business management took the 1992 champions straight into insolvency and relegation. Two months before the end of the 2008–09 season Newcastle owner Mike Ashley seemed set to pull off the same sad feat.

A few rungs further down the ladder, in the shadow of the big floodlights, even more ugly things occurred at the very height of the football boom between 1998 and 2002. In March 2002 two property developers, Mark Guterman and Alex Hamilton, bought debt-ridden Wrexham AFC for £50,000. Three months later the club purchased the freehold to its stadium, the Racecourse Ground, from a brewery for £300,000. The property was immediately transferred to one of Hamilton's companies. In June 2003, club chairman Hamilton decreed that the club should from now on pay £30,000 rent per year for the ground. A year later, Hamilton gave the club notice to quit. He wanted to sell the Racecourse Ground, Wrexham's home since 1872, to a supermarket chain for up to £20 million. The club would receive a third of the price obtained.

In December 2004 the club went into insolvency and the administrator who was appointed appealed against the property deal in court. The judge eventually ruled that Hamilton had been derelict in his duty as club chairman, and that the Racecourse Ground had to return to the ownership of the club. The fans raised more than £200,000 for a takeover. Instead, two local businessmen bought the club, which found itself relegated to the Conference in 2008.

The goings-on at Chesterfield, the fourth-oldest league club in the country (founded 1866), were no less brazen. In summer 2000 a young Sheffield entrepreneur, Darren Brown, took over the Third Division club and made the customary promises to the fans: new players, promotion, success. Brown stuck to his word. Chesterfield signed a succession of expensive players, and sixth months later were heading the table. But then cheques suddenly started bouncing and wages went unpaid. It transpired that Brown had used £800,000 of the club's money for his own purposes. In September 2005 a court found him guilty of theft and false accounting and he was sentenced to four years in prison.

Wimbledon's move from South London to the commuter town of Milton Keynes, about sixty miles to the north-west, was perfectly legitimate, but that was cold comfort for the supporters of the 'Crazy Gang'. In 1991 the long-time owner, a Lebanese businessman called Sam Hammam, had sold the Plough Lane ground to a supermarket for £8 million. The club sublet Crystal Palace's Selhurst Park as its home ground. In 1997 Wimbledon were bought by a Norwegian consortium, and in 2002 an FA commission allowed the club, by then practically bankrupt and relegated to the First Division, to move to Milton Keynes. Out of frustration, the Wimbledon fans declared their old football club dead and re-founded it as AFC Wimbledon in the lowest amateur league. The new 'Dons' have won promotion four times since 2003, their average gate is 3,500, and the supporters would not be supporters if they did not dream of an assault on the top flight. The small Kingsmeadow ground in the suburb of Kingston was purchased in 2005 for £3 million and renamed The Fans' Stadium. The money was raised by donations and a sale of club shares to the supporters. 'Our structure is such that the members' trust will always have the majority share, and our fate will never be decided by outsiders,' said chief executive Kris Stewart.

AFC Wimbledon is a giant among the amateur clubs in

south-west London, and they take their social responsibilities seriously. They organise football training for local schools and holiday camps. Even the shirts are produced locally. There are children's and youth teams, and a women's side – twenty-five teams in total. Almost all the officials work as volunteers. During the summer break the fans have repainted the stadium and organised music evenings in the club bar. 'We're a real club, created by the fans, for the fans,' says Stewart, the godfather of this remarkable renaissance. But he dismisses any talk of a 'football fairy tale'. 'Fairy tales have happy endings. We've got something much better – a future.'

When in summer 2005, following the sale of their club to the Glazer brothers, disappointed Manchester United fans banded together to form FC United of Manchester, they used the example of the London club. The new FCUM's first fixture was against AFC Wimbledon in the Supporters Direct Cup. Each home game of this fan-assembled team is cheered on by a few thousand supporters at Gigg Lane, the ground they share with League Two side Bury FC.

Colin Hendrie, spokesman for the Independent Manchester United Supporters Association (IMUSA), is one of the disgruntled dissidents. 'At the start of the 2005–06 season I returned my Old Trafford season ticket,' he said. 'I prefer watching FC United; it's more fun.' This is not just a decision of the heart. Hendrie and many other fans hope to bring the Glazers to their knees with a stadium and mer-chandising boycott. The Americans' controversial business model – more than a third of the loan for the takeover of United was passed on to the club, and overnight, the best-run club in the business had become a debt-ridden concern with a lot less financial leeway – is chiefly reliant on increasing revenue from ticket sales and merchandising. 'We must ensure that the costing falls through and that the club goes bust,' Hendrie said. 'Then our supporters' trust with its thirty-two thousand members could take it over.' This is no easy undertaking. Hendrie and those like him find themselves in a dilemma, especially emotionally. 'United is my club and I want it to win. But it would be better if it were unsuccessful, because then the Glazers would have to do without the Champions League millions.' United FC's position has become more difficult in the wake of Man Utd's renewed success on and off the pitch.

So that others are spared this torment, Hendrie would like to see a new law that made supporter ownership compulsory, at least up to a certain percentage. Supporters Direct also advocates such an amendment. Fan representatives feel there is a momentum building. 'Clubs in the lower divisions who had their backs to the wall at the end of the boom years have had a change of heart,' claims Supporters Direct chairman Phil French. 'The owners used to see trusts as a threat. But people are realising that the financial input and the involvement of supporters are vital to securing the clubs' future.'

The demise of old, traditional clubs such as Chesterfield, Stockport County, Rushden and Diamonds and Brentford turned out to be a blessing in disguise: the clubs were taken over by the fans. Ten others are now also under trust ownership (by March 2009), including Notts County, the oldest professional club. Today there are 140 supporters' trusts in England, Scotland and Wales. French confidently predicts that the majority of English clubs will be owned by their fans by 2020. Even the Premier League could soon become fan-owned, he thinks. 'We're not talking here about an anti-capitalist model,' French insists. 'A club that belongs to its supporters can work well with sponsors and investors, and be successful. Anybody who doesn't believe this only has to look at Barcelona.'

There is one big success that Supporters Direct can be proud of already: thanks to its work, and to the controversial takeover of Manchester United, the public seem much more ready for a democratisation of the structures, and alert to the dangers of commercialisation. 'We're no longer going to let ourselves be abused as customers, and neither are we going to watch companies milk the clubs' assets – players and grounds,' French says calmly, but determinedly.

The message is getting heard. Times are changing. After the hedonistic consumer revolution of the nineties, when everything just went forwards and upwards, there is a new consensus developing that one has to get back to the game's roots, to a time when club chairmen would not dare to refer to their fans as 'customers'. England, where the game is marketed and staged to perfection, might just become the nucleus of a new social football revolution.

A lot will ride on the severity of the recession. You could argue that the Premier League has been run like a giant Ponzi scheme in recent years. Clubs were spending money they didn't have in the expectation that another owner would come along to sort out the mess. Without any fresh inward investment, middle-sized clubs like Everton or Bolton could soon feel the pinch. Who will be left holding the baby when the sugar daddies have lost their wad and gone home again? The supporters, who else.

'It sounds utopian, but it's happening,' French says. 'We're seeing fan-owned clubs recovering their long-neglected position in the community. Clubs are offering their members healthcare, and they're getting involved in schools and leisure programmes.' The club is becoming what it once used to be: a counterpart to the gentlemen's club; a club for the small man. A third place between work and home, not unlike a pub in its function. A place where the immense English thirst for identification, pride and community is quenched.

CHAPTER 10

Around the World, Around the World

Grey, the sky is grey again. The colour is somewhere between *Sciurus carolinensis* and those itchy, smelly blankets you find on your seat on charter flights. There is none of that late-summer golden brilliance over the capital today; the air is heavy and sticky. Although it is Sunday, the roads are clogged. Traffic crawls forward; everything is a scramble for the next fraction of an inch.

Every few hundred yards white posters outside pubs and restaurants advertise 'The Red Fight' – Liverpool against Manchester United. The match between the arch-rivals from the north-west is on television at every street corner here. It is *the* game of the year, and has been so for the last twenty-five years. In this metropolis of ten million people there are supporters of the Reds and supporters of the Reds. You can comfortably forget Chelsea and Arsenal. Niche clubs, they are.

Three hours before kick-off, young people are thronging through the streets with horns and trumpets, making noise, creating a buzz. The majority of United supporters have turned up in blue today – their team is playing away. The masses are being drawn to a gigantic multi-purpose hall where the game is being shown on a large screen. There is room for at least 7,000 people; almost all the seats are taken two hours before kick-off. For safety reasons, the fans are fastidiously separated. On the left, Liverpool supporters; on the right, United. Three presenters are up on the stage, doing the old hip-hop concert routine to see who can make more noise. Beer is being sold outside the hall. The demand is moderate. Everybody appears to be in a good mood. You can feel the tension, but no aggression. And why should there be? After all, we are not in England, but Bangkok.

The BEC Tero Hall, a pointy concrete mountain, is located within the Suan Lum night bazaar, a labyrinth of restaurants and stalls that sell the kind of stuff only tourists buy, next to Lumpini Park Thai-Boxing Stadium. Around twenty other large venues in Bangkok are transmitting the game today. The city's inhabitants have been getting excited about it for weeks, as if it were a cup final. ESPN, who hold the rights to the Premier League in America and large parts of Asia, are sponsoring the event. A television crew has travelled here specially; the cameras switch live to us before the kick-off. The Thais get the signal from the stage to turn up the volume. They shout, hit those white plastic clubs together and stamp with their feet. The cacophony is a bit disconcerting.

There is no doubt that they take things very seriously here. The three most renowned football journalists are asked on the stage to predict the outcome of the match. And then we are at Anfield. A commentator reads out the line-ups and the substitutes; people applaud enthusiastically. The game is starting. The game is supposed to be starting. But . . . nothing whatsoever happens. Both teams are using a 4-5-1 system, which is all the rage at the beginning of the 2005–06 season, but only works for Mourinho's Chelsea. They are stepping on one another's feet; the ball rarely makes it to either penalty area. The half-time whistle comes as a great relief. The game is a 'stinker', as the English would say – a total disappointment. Sixty minutes and one and a half goal-scoring opportunities later it still says 0–0 on the scoreboard. The Thai commentator had a better game, apparently. He adorned the few points of the game with witty remarks that went down well with the audience. (When Liverpool's Djimi Traore was brought on late in the game – in itself quite funny, you could argue – he shouted with mock excitement, 'Yes, of course, he wants to get a game, too!')

You sense the collective exhaustion. Everybody seems to lack the strength to leave the hall; people have to drag themselves out of their seats and to the exit. Thousands of litres of built-up adrenalin have not been able to find an outlet in big emotions. Now all of it is slowly seeping back into their bodies. It is not a good feeling.

Metha Punwaratorn shrugs his shoulders. He cannot think of anything to say. Great games get even better if you talk about them a lot; rubbish ones, on the other hand, are best deleted from the short-term memory as quickly as possible. Every thought, every word that you waste now is painful. Before the game, Metha, twenty-two, had been in good spirits, and expecting victory. A victory for Rafael Benítez's side, naturally. Metha is a member of the largest Reds fan club, and he writes a column for the influential website Liverpool.in.th (Liverpool in Thailand). His particular organisation has 10,000 members; he estimates the total number of Liverpool supporters in Thailand to be three million. The men from Merseyside are the most popular club, just beating United, but way ahead of Arsenal and Chelsea. Bolton and Manchester City also have a following, it turns out, because they recently played in the Premier League Asian Cup in Bangkok. Everton are popular because the Blues have a Thai sponsor: Chang

Beer. But Liverpool are the undisputed darlings of the Thai football cognoscenti. Why?

'Games have been shown here on television for thirty years,' Metha says. 'And back then Liverpool were just invincible. The Thai people adopted the team.' Unlike the Japanese, who are primarily fans of individual players and only have relatively fleeting connections to the clubs, the Thais behave like 'real' football fans. 'We're the second generation; many of us follow the club their father supported,' Metha says. United's popularity stems from their dominance in the nineties, when many younger Thai people discovered football. For obvious reasons, Chelsea is an attractive club for new supporters, whereas Arsenal, curiously, still suffer from a bad reputation. 'In the eighties and nineties they were seen as a boring team,' Metha says. 'Nobody wanted to support them.' In view of this consciousness of tradition, marketing men talk of a mature market for football. Thailand is far more advanced than China or Japan, in this respect, where the fascination is with the superstars. From a purely economic viewpoint, however, those countries are still seen as potentially far more lucrative.

'The original football shirts are just too expensive for the people here,' says Pirayu Chuenkul. 'You can get fake ones for a few baht. Manchester United had to close its club shop.' Yesterday, Chuenkul was on stage as an expert in the BEC Tero Hall. He is a football journalist with *Star Sport*, one of four daily publications devoted entirely to the Premier League. Its publishing group, Siam Sport, also publishes a specialist sports betting paper, even though gambling is illegal here. The media group is so successful that it will soon be moving into a new headquarters costing several million baht, with its own helicopter landing pad. Chuenkul shows me a model of the new tower block. It stands in the conference room between piles of football books that include Lothar Matthäus's biography *Der Leitwolf* (in German) and other classics of the genre.

'English football has all the first-mover advantages – it was the first to appear on television,' he says. 'Italian, Spanish and German football lag way behind in popularity. That's also to do with the kick-off times: Spain and Italy play when it's the middle of the night here.' The English are more flexible. Since the end of the 1990s many top games have been scheduled to start at midday. In the past this used to happen on police advice – it meant fans would not have time to get slaughtered before kick-off – but nowadays the marketing departments are in charge. Midday matches take place at prime-time in Asia. Even the regular three p.m. slot is more convenient than either La Liga or Serie A, where the best games are scheduled in the evenings. Besides the 'Red Fight', this September weekend sees no fewer than five more Premier League games shown live in Thailand.

Pirayu is far less cynical than the Europeans about English and Spanish clubs setting out on sales tours through Asia. 'The fans know that it's about money, but they don't care. They want the teams to come to them, they want to see their heroes close up; after all they can't go to England. They feel very honoured to have the clubs here.' He reckons mere participation in a friendship tournament in July 2005 brought both Bolton and Blackburn several thousand new fans who will stick with them for life, poor souls.

Although Metha receives no support from Liverpool FC, and has to find information for his columns on the BBC, *Guardian* and *Liverpool Echo* websites, the supporters feel they are taken seriously and are well looked after by their English icons. 'Many fans are girls,' says Metha's girlfriend, Fai, 'and the Liverpool players write very nice letters back.' Do they?

Anfield's marketing department must employ one enthusiastic Thai who delights young female admirers of Steven Gerrard and Xabi Alonso with flowery prose. Unfortunately, the club would not comment. They seem very guarded about their ingenious service for supporters.

The Thai embassy in Berlin are also reluctant to talk about Thaksin Shinawatra's love for the Reds. In May 2004 the then prime minister tried unsuccessfully to secure a thirty per cent share in the club for $100 million. 'Many of our products need a brand, and Liverpool is one we can use on the global market,' he said at the time. 'It is an established club with great popularity in Asia.' Many Thais supported the move – their country's investment would have filled them with pride – but even among the local Liverpool fans there was not clear majority support. It was not so much that Shinawatra, a multimillionaire who is often likened to Silvio Berlusconi on account of his media empire, had declared himself a big Manchester United fan in 1997, but that the prime minister wanted to use taxpayers' money for the acquisition.

'It was a PR stunt,' Pirayu says, 'all meant for self-promotion.' As a seasoned Liverpool fan he was happy that the deal did not come off. 'Stay away from my club! We're not professional enough to run a Premier League side.'

The opposition speculated that Shinawatra wanted to divert attention from the civil-war-like situation in the south of the country at the time. It's quite possible. In August 2005 Home Secretary Kongsak Wantana announced a new measure to pacify the insurgent Muslims in the region: 500 television sets with free access to football for the local tea houses. 'Most children love sport, but they can't afford to watch it at home,' he stated in a press conference. 'So we're giving them what they love. Hopefully this will solve the problem.' Over 800 people had by then died in the area in clashes with security forces. Kongsak's optimism did not appear to be totally unfounded, however. After all, as we know, even Osama Bin Laden enjoys watching the Premier League in his spare time. In 1994 he reportedly watched the Gunners four times at Highbury and bought his son a shirt from the fan shop.

A Reuters reporter who visited the disputed province a few weeks after Kongsak's announcement encountered scepticism, though. 'It's not a good idea,' one Haji Mustafa Bin Haji Abdul Latif, tea house owner in the village of Ban Sawo Hilir, was quoted as saying. 'The children would do nothing but watch television, and they'd forget their schoolbooks and the Koran.' At the same time, however, all his customers professed their love for Liverpool or Manchester United to the journalists, and immediately started a heated debate about the strengths of respective star players.

In the meantime, Shinawatra was happy to discover his admiration for yet another northern club. In 2007 he took over Manchester City. The supporters did not mind ignoring his record of human rights abuses but did get concerned when the Thai froze his assets in the wake of a corruption trial in 2008. In classic City fashion, the club was left with the poorest billionaire in the world in charge, until the rulers of Abu Dhabi turned the City of Manchester Stadium into Middle Eastlands. Liverpool are next in line for a sheikh-up. FIFA might as well forget about their own Club World Cup – the Premier League is precisely that. The first truly international domestic competition.

There is no escaping the Premier League. Its attraction is irresistible, particularly in emerging countries beset by cultural inferiority complexes and a yearning desire for international recognition. 'Many Thais seem to think that the Premiership, with its wealthy international stars, confers a global status upon those who follow it,' Will Pryce wrote in the *Observer* after a visit to Bangkok in 2000. 'As one fan put it to me, by supporting Liverpool, Thailand itself became a player.' If Liverpool won a trophy the whole country could rejoice, because Thailand as a nation had won, too. Pryce continued, '[Thailand has] the ambition to be world-class, to match the developed world in some field. Premiership clubs can do this for you. By supporting Liverpool, some Thais felt instantly involved in a sophisticated western culture.'

It is not the actual strength of the Premier League that is crucial here, but that of English football as a brand. The Asian fan does not have to buy anything. All they have to do is align themselves with a club from the 'best league in the world' and the glamour of the globe's biggest spectacle shines back on them.

Those who watch the game can feel themselves to be true supporters even without wearing an original shirt on their chest. After all, just turning on the television is of direct economic benefit to their favourite team. In 2008–09, the Premier League was earning an astonishing £208 million per year from foreign rights alone; the Bundesliga, by comparison, was selling its international rights for approximately £30 million in the same year. In 201 countries, 1,400 hours of English football are watched every week in 613 million households. The average match is seen by eighty million people. In China, 360 million people watched the live transmission of a match between Manchester City and Everton in January 2003, when two Chinese footballers were in action.

Television and merchandising revenue from abroad allow the clubs to buy star players; these in turn attract more fans; and this creates a self-perpetuating 'virtuous cycle' (Richard Scudamore). And people like success. Manchester United, the team of the nineties and noughties, have 333 million supporters worldwide according to a 2008 poll – one in every twenty people on the planet. Only a tiny fraction of them, David Gill has said, are currently customers, so the potential for growth is considerable. The endgame is, of course, the direct marketing of broadcasting rights.

In summer 2005, 27,000 fans of English football from around the world, including Mongolia, were asked what they liked about the Premier League. For 57 per cent it was the players, 47 per cent said 'the goals', and 31 per cent 'the style of play' (those surveyed were allowed to give multiple answers). There were strong regional differences. The cult of star players is strongest in Africa and Asia, whereas for almost half of those surveyed from South America the style of football was most important. Sadly the survey did not define more precisely what the global audiences understood by that. Are toughness, fair play and speed the decisive attributes? It is safe to make this assumption.

'Honestly, the referees are a very important factor,' says Martin Mazur, football journalist with *El Grafico* in Argentina. 'I'm not trying to say that people will watch because of them, but they do their bit because in our country people are fed up to the teeth with yellow and red cards being given out for nothing – and I mean nothing. The English game, on the other hand, is full of battles, dangerous tackles and confrontations, but at the end everything calms down again. It's the physical game that we like so much.'

Mazur has written an article about Juan Manuel Pons, chief commentator for Fox Sports. The station, owned by Rupert Murdoch, has the broadcasting rights in South America. Pons is famous for composing his own songs for various players. He does not scream 'Goooooooooooool!' but sings the name of the scorer to the tunes of Beatles, Stones or U2 hits. 'I think the Premier League also benefits from its Englishness, from

the strong association between pop music and youth culture,'
says Mazur. 'No one watches Juventus versus Milan because
the game is being played in Italy. But Manchester United
against Arsenal, that's England. And England is interesting.'

Not just for the Argentinians. The German sports television
channel DSF has from the outset accompanied its Premier
League reports with chart hits from England, and thus made
an obvious connection between the two. The Premier League
is pop. The Premier League is hip. In countries that have
their own healthy football culture but see English football
as their 'second league', people consciously choose the Premier
League as a modern lifestyle product. Even before the influx of
international stars made it relevant for ever more countries, it
enjoyed the advantage of relative accessibility. People
understand the language, at least a little.

In a study of Scandinavian fans of English clubs, the
Swedish academic Bo Reimer found that they considered
football very much as an element of British popular culture –
and the latter has been considered highly attractive since the
1960s. 'This is why football trips to England became incredibly
popular. Over the course of a weekend in London, Liverpool,
Manchester or Newcastle, Scandinavians could attend a game,
and then go to pubs, the theatre, a disco or a rock concert,'
he writes.

Drama on the pitch combined with strong, genuine
emotions in the stands produces the best-selling formula
known to capitalism: English football is a product that does
not seem like a product. It is 'authentic'. And, at the same
time, somehow youthful, cool and current. This is due to the
pace, the continual movement, and the frantic switches
between attack and defence.

'Sociologists in several countries have found that increasing
wealth and increasing education bring a sense of tension

about time,' James Gleick writes in his book *Faster: The Acceleration of Just About Everything*. 'We believe we possess too little of it: that is the myth we now live by.' Because our time is so precious, everything has to be faster. Food, travel, communication. Speed is no longer the means to an end, but a highly desirable commodity in itself. A direct flight costs more than a journey with a stopover. If you want your shirt cleaned overnight or your photos printed within the hour, you pay a supplement. Everything to save time. Twenty-first-century consumerism demands instant gratification. The non-stop action of the Premier League gives it to us.

'If the Bundesliga is like a normal train, football here is a bullet train,' Jens Lehmann said of his experience in Britain. There are actually fewer goals than in Germany, but the perceived number of incidents is higher. 'You're right in the game the moment you come on,' Fredi Bobic raved after his first outing for Bolton Wanderers in January 2002. 'I've never had so many touches inside the box in a match as I did in those forty-five minutes.' There is no English equivalent of *Abtastungsphase*, the cagey, cautious opening exchanges. Or maybe it simply does not last that long. In September 2003, Blackburn's Markus Babbel accidentally broke the ankle of Liverpool's Milan Baros with the very first tackle of the game.

Nowhere is the acceleration of everyday life as visible as in the media. These days eighties blockbusters such as *Star Wars* or the Indiana Jones films, admonished at the time for their frenzied, hyperactive editing, seem leisurely, almost slow. Video clips and advertisements race against one another. Who can pack more cuts into one single second? If people from the nineteenth century watched early evening television their eyeballs would probably give up after a few minutes. Our capacity to process visual data has increased by the same rate our attention span has become shorter.

Gleick writes, 'Every television programmer works in the shadow of the awareness that the audience is armed.' They have a remote control in their hand, 'an instant polling device, continually measuring dissatisfaction or flagging attention'. Is it boring yet? Am I still paying attention? English football has the right, manic rhythm for the post-MTV generation.

Somehow, even a boring game is made to look dynamic thanks to the camera positions, which tend to be closer to the pitch, and the angle is steeper than in Germany. Sky, the broadcaster that has revolutionised football in England with its money and know-how, does not like to discuss its production techniques. Secrets of the trade. The boys from Isleworth in West London certainly do a good job, however, as their pictures are swooned over across the world. The slow-motion sequences are spectacular; the picture is incredibly sharp yet has the kind of softness one associates with Hollywood productions. It is television that looks like cinema. Big-screen cinema.

Probably the biggest difference to German TV football, however, is the soundtrack. Sky cranks up the volume of the crowd; you can hear every heckle, every dirty little song. The commentator keeps pace with the tempo of the game, like a German radio reporter. The journalistic ethos in Germany demands distance. It is not uncommon for a commentator to analyse the reasons for an unsuccessful attack before it is actually over. On English television, on the other hand, commentary must sound as intense and close to the game as possible. To commentate on a match in England demands dexterity and pace – you have to keep up with play, just like the referee. Names of players are uttered every time they touch the ball; no attack goes unmentioned. The faster the match, the more the man behind the microphone will talk. His rising crescendo acts to increase the excitement. The viewer is grabbed by the neck and dragged violently down on to the pitch, into the Tempodrome. The speaker does not pause for breath. He does not give you time. In other words, he creates a frenzy that is not always actually there. Something is always happening, even when nothing is happening. When things do really slow down, ex-footballers jump in with their observations. Many other countries keep the English commentary in their broadcast. It is all part of the overall experience.

In a world that is gathering pace by the nanosecond, time is not only a luxury, but a negative status symbol as well: the less you have of it, the greater the prestige. Everybody wants to look as busy as they possibly can. A footballer needs time, but he does not in any circumstances want to play in a league that gives him a lot of time on the ball, because that suggests a lack of quality.

Speed, pace, power, competition, the pressure to produce and the tension between individuality and collectivism (tactics) – English football appears modern because it is all about negotiating modernity. Purists may lament that, at this devilish pace, only a very small number of teams are able to play a cultured passing game, and complain that beauty and speed do not go well together. But who cares?

Pirayu, the *Star Sport* man from Bangkok, says, 'The Premier League is much more exciting than other leagues; more happens in the games. And we like the fact that the players are proud and fight for their teams. I think it resonates with our national psyche: we're peaceful, but if somebody has a go at us we don't shy away from battle.' For Metha, too, the 'aggression on the pitch' is the most exciting feature. A ruffian like Wayne Rooney – 'we call him the wild pig' – was admired precisely for his tendency to get violent, he says.

'The spirit of fair play, however, is also extremely important,' Pirayu thinks. 'Thai people do not like cheats; we don't like seeing someone trying to fool the referee. In England that happens less often. The game is unadulterated, somehow more honest.' Premier League players are also seen as incorruptible, and for millions of Asian gamblers that is the real, key criterion. The Thai national league cannot be trusted in this regard. Only a few thousand spectators attend the games; they are hardly shown on television at all.

We are standing outside the large hall, surrounded by souvenir stands and shops offering copied DVDs, and mobile food stalls where chicken skewers are turning into charcoal. It has got dark. Fai, the Thai Scouser, looks less exhausted than most of those who have watched 'The Red Fight'. She smiles contentedly. 'It's a shame we didn't win,' she says, 'but it was a good battle. And a fair result. I thought it was nice that the players swapped shirts after the game and embraced each other.'

That might well be another reason for English football's incredible success: its battles invariably end on a conciliatory note. There is an optimism here, a great metaphysical truth, casually told. In spite of different (club) colours, finances, results and positions in the tables, there is more that connects us than separates us. Is not 'fair play' another way of saying we're all equal under the law and in the eyes of God?

'Yes, maybe,' Fai smiles shyly, 'but what I like best of all is that you see the players' nice bodies at the end of the game.'

CHAPTER 11

Two World Wars, Minus Two World Cups

They say Germans don't have a sense of humour. I don't find that funny.

Henning Wehn

The train was rattling sluggishly through the darkness. This was not one of those shiny ICEs (Inter City Expresses) but, disappointingly by German standards, a collection of ramshackle cargo carriages hastily strung together to make up one of the many WM-Sonderzüge (World Cup special trains) that criss-crossed the country throughout the tournament.

Our compartment did not have any seats but then it was long past midnight and people were by now happy to cower on the floor, next to the bike rails. One tall young man in his twenties, however, was standing up, defiantly. He was wearing trainers, camouflage shorts, an England replica shirt and a green 'Tommy' toy soldier helmet. Once the doors closed he treated his unsuspecting audience of a few dozen tired football supporters to the good old 'Ten German Bombers' song. His girlfriend, a petite blonde, looked on a little embarrassed at first, then decided to join in out of loyalty, together with the predominantly English passengers.

The tall guy bellowed out all the verses at the top of his increasingly coarse voice. When the last Luftwaffe plane had finally been shot down, the silence promised a peaceful continuation of the journey. But then he started again, from the very top. Fewer people joined in this time. Tommy was singing with his eyes closed now. This was becoming a test of endurance for everyone involved.

He swayed like a notched oak tree but did not fall. Ten German bombers were brought down by the 'RAF from England' once again, before German beer did what the slow pace of the ride could not do: the giant's knees buckled, and he decided that continuing the recital in a horizontal position was more advisable.

Tommy tried to summon the spirit of the Blitz one more time but he could no longer fight off the drowsiness. Soon he was snoring on his back. The whole carriage was laughing, mostly out of relief. Two other England supporters took up the baton soon after with a hearty rendition of '5–1, even Heskey scored', at which point three German lads, who had sat quietly in the corner before, were moved to retaliate with a meek, 'We won the last game at Wembley.' The banter went back and forth for a good hour before the train pulled into Frankfurt and spat out the bedraggled human mess.

England's forgettable 2–0 victory over Trinidad and Tobago in Nürnberg earlier that evening was already forgotten. It had taken a Peter Crouch goal in the eighty-first minute to break the deadlock; an unconvincing England had plucked victory from thin air. *An den Haaren herbeigezogen* ('pulled from hair') is the equivalent German expression, and it was never more apt than here: Crouch had yanked the ponytail of poor Brent Sancho just before his goal.

In those tired, dismally uneventful group games, the England supporters in the stands gave a much better account of themselves than Eriksson's men on the pitch. Despite much talk about a clampdown, ticket-touting had de facto been legalised; the stadiums were dominated by the white and red of St George. Football was coming home, the RAF were doing their bit, the Queen was being saved, Heskey scored and there was always a Great Escape to cheer, even if England could never quite escape their own mediocrity. The old war film ditty, another classic at England matches, had an added resonance in Germany – alas one to which the natives were completely oblivious. They simply enjoyed the tune and hummed along, the way they had innocently co-opted 'Football's Coming Home' at Euro 96. You could say they did not get it. Which is exactly what they thought of the English, of course.

The 2006 World Cup was to alter many preconceptions, but the fundamental misunderstanding at the heart of Anglo-German football relations remained unchanged. The average German fan has a basic grasp of English but he has no idea what his counterparts are on about. Leaving the war aside for a moment, you may feel that '5–1 in Munich' is straightforward enough, a piece of harmless, unpolitical banter designed to rile the opposition. Problem is, the Germans are just not riled by it.

To be sure, getting beaten so comprehensively in 2001 hurt. *Bild*'s triumphalism (BYE-BYE ENGLAND – WE'RE GOING TO THE WORLD CUP WITHOUT YOU) on the eve of the match was as ill-advised as Franz Beckenbauer's '5–4 win for Germany' prediction in the same paper, based on a like-for-like comparison of the players. Two days later the tabloid was lamenting 'a first-class execution' and a demotion to the game's also-rans. 'We don't stand a chance against the truly great football nations any more,' claimed sports editor Alfred Draxler.

The quality papers concentrated on the shambolic German defence – exposed as 'at best average in international terms' (*Süddeutsche Zeitung*) – and 'the lack of stability and individual class' (*Frankfurter Allgemeine Zeitung*) in Rudi Völler's side. England's performance was seen in realistic terms. 'In ten years, people may say that Munich was the beginning of a great English football team,' wrote Ronald Reng in *Süddeutsche*. 'But as of now, the stunning result has not changed the assessment. England were a promising young team before [the game], and they are no more than that today. They are, like Germany, who also failed at the [2000] Euros, a good but immature side who are still in the process of being built.'

The Monday after the match, Oliver Kahn's gloves were smouldering on the front page of the *Mirror* ('RIP arrogant, clinical, penalty-scoring and downright bloody irritating German football'). The tabloid nearly duped the German keeper into accepting a cup filled with football's version of the Ashes. They had told the German FA he was being awarded 'a fair-play trophy' but were unlucky to find only his Bayern Munich deputy Stefan Wessels at the club's training ground when they turned up to take a photo. The (forced) symbolism of the burned sports equipment was naturally lost on the Germans.

Munich, the heaviest home defeat in seventy years, was a major embarrassment and stoked the fires of post-millennial *Fussball-Angst*. But the pain was too transient to amount to a traumatic experience. As Germany qualified for the 2002 World Cup and even made it to the final in Yokohama (somehow), the England defeat became an irrelevance. This was no surprise. In fact, we consider all qualification matches as something of an irrelevance. Maybe we have been spoilt by our relatively unblemished record – Germany have been present at every major tournament since Euro 68 – but results in qualifiers, even the very good and the very bad, have never left much of an impression on the football nation's collective memory. These games are simply seen as annoying obstacles on the path to the tournament proper.

Throughout the eighties and nineties, before the commercialisation of the game led to an emphasis on entertainment value, Germany's qualifiers and friendlies were notoriously dull affairs. Turning on the style against the likes of Albania was in fact considered unprofessional by the players. The only pride they showed was in succeeding with minimum effort. And who could blame them? Germans were (and are) only ever interested in performances at the actual championships. This strict – you might call it pedantic – hierarchy of importance is by no means unique to our country. Ask an Italian, Spaniard or Dutchman to name three great, historic performances in the preliminary rounds and they will stare at you blankly. At best, they will remember the last campaign.

A German TV programme would never have included Dietmar Hamann's goal at Wembley in 2000 in a 'Best of the World Cup' show – for us, that would have been preposterous. In the run-up to Germany 2006, however, the Munich goals and Beckham's last-minute belter against Greece were all over UK screens, followed by assorted talking heads who explained that the 5–1 result meant so much 'because it was against Germany, and in the World Cup'. A German supporter will tell you the exact opposite: Munich had no bearing whatsoever on the World Cup. More importantly for the argument of this book, the fact that it was England who had administered the punishment did not arouse any special feelings, either. It might come as a surprise to some, but from where we are sitting England–Germany games do not loom large in our footballing consciousness. There simply is no meaningful England–Germany rivalry to speak of.

Firstly, Britain as a country is generally well liked and admired. London is the most popular weekend destination for German tourists after Paris and Rome. The UK is seen as tolerant, modern and cultured, its people as polite, funny and engagingly eccentric. English football has also, by and large, been very warmly received ever since the game swept across a newly unified Germany in the late nineteenth century. *Das Mutterland des Fussballs* ('the motherland of football') is revered for the pace and (mostly) controlled violence of its matches, for the attitude of its players and supporters, and for its sense of fair play.

The 1966 World Cup changed nothing. Germany had not beaten England in eleven attempts before. The German players went into the Wembley final as underdogs in their own minds. They were not overly disappointed with the outcome. As the TV footage testifies, defeat was accepted in good grace by Franz Beckenbauer and co., despite the dubious third goal and people on the pitch for the fourth. It took a few glasses of champagne at the official banquet for Helmut Schön's men to challenge Swiss referee Gottfried Dienst. 'You've been betrayed!' cried *Bild*, but life went on without German yobs descending on Dienst's home town of Basle or an orchestrated hate campaign against linesman Tofik Bahramov.

Any sense of injustice was quickly tempered by subsequent wins over England in two epic, classic games (Mexico 1970, Wembley 1972) and the arrival of silverware in 1972 and 1974. By the time England and Germany met again in Turin for the 1990 World Cup semi-final, Germans were mostly unaware that their opponents saw this as a very special occasion. England had barely flickered on the international radar in the intervening years; they had only crossed swords with Germany once in earnest since 1970, in a drab, inconsequential 0–0 draw at the 1982 World Cup. As far as Beckenbauer's 1990 side were concerned they had already won their particular grudge match – against the Dutch in the second round – and Italy's defeat by Argentina in the other semi-final the night before had mercifully ensured they wouldn't face their other bête noire. The Turin game was just another semi-final, their sixth in seven competitions. Had it not been for the acute fear of hooligan violence, Germany might as well have been facing Cameroon.

Holland or Italy, now that would have been a very different story. German football rivalries with these two nations are felt keenly, mutually, and the Second World War is merely the starting point. In a nutshell, the Dutch resent us for invading their country, stealing their bikes and denying their brilliant 1974 World Cup team of Johan Cruyff et al. their destiny. They bemoan our overtly functional approach and lack of creativity. They see us as arrogant. We see them as sore losers who keep going on about flair in the face of constant under-achievement. Oh, and they are famously arrogant, too. According to German football mythology, the 1974 final comeback occurred when the Oranjes, 1–0 up at the time, started to make fun of our side with provocative flicks.

Deep down, each side knows that the other has a point. That is why it grates so much. Secretly, we would like to be a bit more like the Dutch, more skilful, more universally popular. And they would certainly not mind a bit more Teutonic *Ergebnisfussball* ('results football'), either. 'In Germany, I became a real man,' said Rafael van der Vaart, the former Hamburg player, at Euro 2008. 'I now know that playing football means winning.' 'First of all, it's important to be secure at the back,' added defender Joris Mathijsen, another HSV player.

With the Italians, it's a similar story of unsatisfied needs and desires. Germans have cast longing, admiring looks across the Alps for as long as anyone can remember. 'Oh yes, the country of the blooming lemon trees!' writes Vicenzo Delle Donne in *Der Lieblingsfeind*, a book about Germany's football rivals. 'This yearning for Italy is almost a popular disease – since Goethe, but before that, too. Famous psychologists have talked of an insidious envy complex.' Psychoanalysing national character is a murky business, but it's probably fair to say that at some unconscious level we begrudge them the beauty of their country and their sun-kissed lives. We worry about the sexual appeal of Italian men and think they don't quite deserve all their good fortune. The (mostly) unspoken assumption is that Italians do not work as hard as we do, are a bit flaky and disorganised. The Italians, on the other hand, think we're humourless kill-joys, obsessed with order. They would welcome a bit more of that boring stability in their own country – but not at the price of turning into Germans, naturally.

There is a saying in Italy that neatly sums up these contrasting attitudes: 'The Germans love the Italians but don't respect them, the Italians respect the Germans but don't love them.'

When it comes to *calcio*, the symmetry is almost as perfect. It is true that German football has long felt neglected and unloved by its southern neighbours, who have, in our eyes, too readily compared winning German teams with *panzeri* (tanks) and the Wehrmacht. In turn, the Italians are rightly aggrieved that knee-jerk allegations of foul play and indiscriminate, hysterical criticism of *catenaccio* (the defensive style) have greeted too many of their successes. Both accusations suggest that wins have really been achieved by illegitimate means.

Our real gripe, however, is with results. Italy always – always – beat us in important World Cup encounters. In club football, our record is equally poor. It's hard for a country that prides itself on delivering when it matters to live with this sense of entrenched inferiority. Attempts to rationalise the situation by zooming in on the Italian male's supposed character flaws betray our helplessness.

Following Italy's 1–0 win over Australia at the 2006 World Cup, a game that was won thanks to a late, controversial penalty, a column in Spiegel Online trotted out the tired clichés. 'The Italian man, let's call him Luigi Forello, is a parasitic life-form,' the piece opened. 'His predominant goal in life is the avoidance of physical effort. His preferred host is "La Mama", who washes his silky socks and cooks spaghetti for him, with plenty of sauce on top . . . When it comes to sport, Luigi is especially sly. You can see it every year on the beaches of the Adriatic. He takes hours to oil his face and slender body, to remove the remnants of fur on his back and cram his less than spectacular privates into swimming trunks that are much too tight. Because he is quickly exhausted, the faintest touch by an opponent is enough for him to go to the ground melodramatically. Still in flight, he looks around to see whether there are enough people in the audience, especially women, who will take pity on him and buck him up again.'

Achim Achilles's column tried to have fun with the stereotypes, to satirise those who cling to them, but it was far too crudely executed to work. It provoked outrage in Italy and condemnation in Germany. Spiegel Online withdrew the offending work from their server with an apology. 'In several passages,' the statement read, 'his column crossed the boundary between good and bad taste. In others, he amassed clichés that, in their sum, led to considerable misunderstanding and anger.'

It is easy to see that raw envy lies at the root of these rivalries, a feeling that is wholly absent in our attitude towards 'England' – both as a team and as country. The Three Lions have been too toothless over the last forty-odd years to cause any resentment or anxiety. Countless computer simulations have convinced us that Hurst's shot never crossed the line, but 1966 did not have the capacity to hurt or unnerve in 2006 – not when Germany had been to four more World Cup and two more European Championship finals in the interim, and won five major competitions. Even in purely aesthetic terms we feel that England has nothing on us. If anything it is the one great football nation less stylish than us on the international stage. And somehow the English always fail to live up to the excitement and standards of attacking football we have come to admire in their league. As a consequence, as a rivalry, England–Germany does not really exist in our book. Or, if you will, it is a bit like England–Scotland: decidedly one-sided.

This is not to say that the dynamic could not change. The digital age, along with the improved skills of the English, has certainly made Germans much more aware in recent years of the strength of feeling across the Channel. This has created a bit of a backlash. Some sections of our media have themselves become obsessed with England–Germany and begun to take a delight in England's failings at international tournaments that goes beyond the usual bounds of Schadenfreude. A detailed knowledge of your hang-ups would undoubtedly make a win over England at a big competition a lot sweeter now than it was in 1990 or 1996.

There is also the matter of the Premier League's increasing dominance in the Champions League, and its appeal to superstars the Bundesliga cannot attract. So far, reaction to this relatively new phenomenon has been positive. Both Jürgen Klinsmann and his successor Jogi Löw have taken the Premier

League's pacy, attacking game as a blueprint for the German national team.

One of the harshest stats the man from Huntington Beach, California, quoted to his new employers Bayern Munich in 2008 was the difference in pace between Germany's top division and the Premier League. In Germany, on average, players retain possession for 2.4 seconds before they pass, Klinsmann calculated, whereas in England a player's time on the ball was only 1.3 seconds. Premier League observers who are unfortunate enough to watch games that do not feature one of the top sides might query the relevance of these numbers without the corresponding tally of all the misplaced passes and hopeful punts towards the corner flag, but most people would agree that the Bundesliga needs to speed things up a bit.

Clubs like Wolfsburg and Hoffenheim have adopted the English management structure, and Franz Beckenbauer has acknowledged that 'the music, the best music, plays in England these days'. However, the gleeful reporting of the effects of the credit crunch on the island's top flight – ENGLAND'S CLUBS IN PANIC was *Stern*'s headline in October 2008 – revealed that adulation is shadowed by jealousy, too. There was a sense that the Premier League was getting its comeuppance: in the eyes of many German supporters its success has merely been 'bought'. But a failure to come to terms with the basic tenets of professional football – money and size do matter – is of course not distinctive to our public discourse. In any case, club football neither excites whole countries nor creates the powerful emotions of a shared experience. It is safe to assume that a genuine England–Germany rivalry is still a few English penalty shoot-out triumphs and open-top bus parades through Pall Mall away.

So neither '5–1, even Heskey scored' nor 'One World Cup' rankled on that train in 2006. But would it have been different if it had been Dutch or Italian fans, our real rivals, doing the singing? The answer is, probably not. In order to understand this strange German lack of concern, one needs to be familiar with one of our most fundamental tenets: *Nach dem Spiel ist vor dem Spiel*, 'after the game is before the game'. This famous aphorism of Sepp Herberger, the World Cup-winning manager of 1954, illustrates perhaps the key cultural difference with English football: in Germany, the past has very little currency.

The democratic, modern West Germany that came into existence in 1949 knew it had to face up to its terrible history in order to establish a better, forward-looking country. But looking back over your shoulder has never been a popular pastime in the Federal Republic of Germany because the things you see there are so very disconcerting. Post-war German society has made a valiant effort to learn from the horrors of the twentieth century, but the expression *Vergangenheitsbewältigung* ('coping with the past') reveals the difficulty of the process.

This introspection has made nostalgia, the fantasy of a past that never was, all but impossible. In our relatively short history as a nation-state – Germany was only unified in 1871 – there is no period that can be held up as a golden age. In cultural life, too, achievements of yesteryear count for very little. There are no OBEs or knighthoods to be won for good deeds. Germany is closer to the USA and its attitude of 'It ain't where you from, it's where you at' (hip-hop MC Rakim): what you are doing now is much more important than what you have done. Call it short-termism, pragmatism or cold-heartedness, but Germany is a place where World Cup and/or European Championship winners cannot dine out on former glory for ever. They can't become successful TV pundits on the strength of one solitary winning goal. There is no after-dinner-speaker circuit and no market for match balls and signed shirts. Most of the former stars wouldn't even get a free drink anywhere. Their heroics aren't forgotten, they simply lack significance. Revelling in past successes (or in glorious failures) is actively discouraged in the game. It's generally seen as pointless, if not counter-productive.

Two years after Stefan Effenberg won the Champions League for Bayern Munich, their first European Cup after a wait of twenty-five years, the fans were booing him in the Olympiastadion. His performances had deteriorated to the point that he was rarely venturing out of the centre circle. The terraces showed him no mercy.

A disregard of games gone by is also evident when supporters are teasing their opposite numbers. 'We won the league at White Hart Lane', an Arsenal favourite whenever they play Spurs, would never be heard in the Bundesliga. For Schalke fans, who missed out on the title in 2001 in traumatic circumstances – they were already celebrating on the pitch before the stadium TV screens showed a decisive last-minute goal from Bayern against Hamburg – being reminded of that day is far less excruciating than the prospect of even more pain in the future. Bayern and Dortmund fans know that, so they goad them with 'You'll never be German champions'.

This refusal to dwell on past defeats extends beyond the pitch. Which finally brings us to the big red elephant in the room, the one with the swastika on its back.

In *Der Lieblingsfeind*, author Christopher Young argues that all the war jokes and Kraut headlines are mostly banter, firmly grounded in the British tradition of pantomime. He quotes Lord Dahrendorf, the German-British sociologist: 'The British love the impossible and the eccentric, and they virtually come into their own when they are not being politically correct, but they don't always appreciate that they could be taken more seriously abroad than they take the world on the other side of the Channel.' Young also notes that nuances of humour are often lost in translation – or completely misinterpreted. One example: the German FA took out a full-page ad in *The Times* the day after the Euro 96 final to thank their English hosts for the successful tournament. The gesture was sincere, but 'many Englishmen mistook it for a slightly wayward form of banter'. The Germans have traditionally erred on the other side. We take matters seriously as a matter of course.

Before the 1966 final the English press was notably reluctant to mention the war; 'Allusions to history were made, of course, but they didn't seem malicious,' writes David Downing. Maybe the war was still too raw a subject to be laughed about. Maybe the young, well-behaved German team simply did not make for good pantomime villains and the Argentinians beat us to it. One columnist from *Bild*, however, still seemed genuinely disturbed by the harmless banter he encountered in the tabloids. 'It's a shame I am not as brazen as some English journalists,' wrote Werner Pietsch with marked despair. 'They behave in complete contrast to the much appreciated, noble English manner of the man in the street. If I wrote in English, I would have salivated over Germany's win against Switzerland [and written that] "eleven Germans skilfully slice up Swiss cheese! [. . .] These guys would be better off skiing, keeping cows or milking some goats." As readers, you would have been surprised and disgusted, just as I am when I open up the English newspapers and read wicked, unsporting comments every day. For the sake of a joke, they make mincemeat out of men and teams. I'm dreading the final between England and Germany.'

We now know that Fleet Street did not do its worst that day and that *Bild*, a paper explicitly modelled on British tabloids by publisher Axel Springer, would soon come down off its high horse. By 1996 they were asking the English side rhetorical questions: 'Why can't you beat your former colonies at cricket?', 'Why can't you pour a proper pint?', 'Why have you never won the European Championship?' Tragically unfunny, unfortunately, but they tried.

Germany's only national tabloid is a monopolist in the fields of vilification and robust language. The lack of competition in the marketplace has sadly seen the paper's tone stuck at base crassness. More often than not, *Bild*'s football coverage lacks the wit, playfulness and sophistication of true banter in the English sense of word. There is little of the twisted genius of 'Up Yours, Delors', for example. In the paper's defence, German is a much more difficult language to work with; it lends itself far less to puns. *Bild* has no ambitions to be too original in any case; it is content to openly patronise its readers with countless *Bild erklärt* ('*Bild* explains') stories instead.

And let's not kid ourselves: our sense of humour is patently less developed than that of the English, who have long made the ability to crack a joke a core provision of social competence. To German ears, it is always striking to hear British politicians, businessmen or even random acquaintances make a real effort to be at least mildly entertaining. Your society ascribes enormous importance to the art of laughter. The writer A. A. Gill thinks this is a displacement activity. 'The English teeter on the edge of not being able to take anything seriously,' he writes in *The Angry Island.* 'The ability to be solemn or even appropriate, reflective or sad in public, is so uncomfortably embarrassing that they're forced to giggle or snigger.'

Be that as it may, go to any German football ground and you will find plenty of rude gestures, swear words and gratuitous insults, but little banter. Unlike English supporters, who are experts in spotting weaknesses and ruthlessly exploiting them – within hours of the news that Chelsea captain John Terry's mother had been arrested for shop-lifting, for instance, Arsenal fans were singing 'She'll be coming out of Tesco's with her dinner in her coat' – German fans confine themselves to the standard repertoire of *Zieht den Bayern den Lederhosen aus* ('Pull down Bayern's leather trousers'), *Wir wollen keine . . . Schweine* ('We don't want you . . . pigs') and *Scheiss Millionäre* ('crap millionaires'). Amid the increasingly powerful ultra-movement on the terraces you get points for choreographed displays and loud chanting, but not for fine wit or well-rounded irony.

German (football) culture is not familiar enough with the concepts of banter and pantomime to know that the best and indeed only possible response to 'Ten German Bombers' is something along the lines of 'If it weren't for the Yanks, you'd all be Krauts'. But we would still be reluctant to sing it because wars and fun do not mix very well in our book. Tellingly, Hans von Plotz, the German ambassador, had to be told by Radio Four host Jim Naughtie that the *News of the World* headline after the 5–1 win in Munich, DON'T MENTION THE SCORE, was a joke. 'It is not our sense of humour,' he replied tartly, adding quickly, 'though we do have one.'

An Englishman might debate this, and not without reason. Here, humour is a weapon that many are prepared to turn on themselves for a laugh; you could argue that this island's special brand of self-deprecating fun is one of its greatest cultural accomplishments. Nothing is off limits, and certainly not the war: in the *Fawlty Towers* episode 'The Germans', which sees Basil goose-stepping and shouting, 'Don't mention the war!' in the vicinity of German tourists, the joke is very much 'about English attitudes to the war and the fact that some people were still hanging on to that rubbish', according to John Cleese.

When he moved to play here, Jürgen Klinsmann understood that a touch of hammy self-parody would endear him to English hearts. He showed up at a press conference with diving goggles and snorkel, then celebrated by diving on to the pitch after scoring his first goal for Spurs. So why can't the Germans get over themselves and laugh along with the English when they conflate football and the war with headlines like WE BEAT THEM IN '45, WE BEAT THEM IN '66, NOW THE BATTLE OF '90 (the *Sun*, next to a cartoon of Hitler shouting 'Victory or the firing squad!' at the German team)? Why can't we have the good grace to poke fun at ourselves, the way losers are supposed to here?

We probably could, if '1945' was merely shorthand for a severe defeat at the hands of the Allies. But the issue is much more complicated. For a start, we feel that the scope, scale, course and ramifications of the Second World War render any analogy with a game obscene. You can, just about, imagine an exchange of 'Well played' / 'Unlucky' between Germans and Allies at the Paris Peace Conference in 1918, but not in 1945.

When we think about and talk of that war, the actual battles take a back seat. They are very much an afterthought, a part of the story that is wholly overshadowed by the incomprehensible monstrosity of the Holocaust and the sheer evil of an ideology that unleashed death on most of Europe. 'The shame and guilt Germans confront daily, more thoroughly and obsessively than probably any other nation on earth' (German ambassador to London Thomas Matussek in 2005) is not the shame and guilt of losing the war, it's the shame and guilt of starting it. With the exception of a tiny minority of incorrigible Nazi sympathisers, we see ourselves – or our progenitors, to be more precise – as perpetrators, not losers.

Victims can dabble with self-deprecating humour if they feel so inclined, but for the country responsible for their plight it is not a genre that lends itself to too many laughs. Belittling the Nazis is very difficult without also belittling their crimes. In his analysis of the media reaction to the 5–1 result, the *Independent*'s David Lister found that Fleet Street's attitudes towards Germany had softened considerably since the 'Achtung Fritz!' excesses of the 1990s. 'The press seems to have turned the corner,' he wrote, 'the war may really be over.' The popularity of 'Ten German Bombers' during 2006 did not necessarily suggest otherwise. Even the most po-faced of Germans was able to shrug his shoulders in the face of such puerile nonsense. But deep down our hearts sank a little every time another plane was shot down because the song corroborated the fear that our visitors had still not grasped the true nature of post-war Germany: we are grateful that we lost the war.

In our history books, May Day is the day the Allies liberated the country – us – from Nazism. In recent years one or two revisionist historians have tried, mostly in vain, to start a debate about 'war crimes': the bombing of Dresden or the treatment of German PoWs. But every right-thinking German knows they owe their good fortune and economic success to the fact that the *Tausendjährige Reich*, Hitler's 1,000-year Reich, was dramatically cut short by the Allies. West Germans are particularly indebted to the benign influence of the Western powers. A quick look over the wall into the German Democratic Republic was enough to see that our lot could have much been worse.

Consequently, West German TV stations thought nothing of screening classic Second World War films like *The Longest Day* (*Der längste Tag*), *The Great Escape* (*Gesprengte Ketten*) or *A Bridge Too Far* (*Die Brücke von Arnheim*). The voices of US and British soldiers were dubbed into German by the country's finest actors, while Wehrmacht soldiers were sometimes left shouting in the pidgin German of Hollywood and Elstree. For us, the Nazis were the villains of the piece, too.

British men raised on a diet of Second World War comics (in which 'Schweinehund!' is just about all the Germans ever say) might assume that we have our own Boy's Own stories – tales of valiant battles in Normandy, perhaps – but German popular culture has concentrated almost exclusively on Nazi crimes against humanity. The only true 'war film' of German provenance, Die Brücke (The Bridge) from 1959, is an anti-war film: it tells the story of seven sixteen-year-old boys who are cynically drafted into battle during the last days of the conflict. All but one of them dies in a futile fight to defend a small, militarily unimportant bridge against the Americans.

German comedians – they do exist – have wisely steered clear of the topic, but what exactly is it that the English find so hilarious about 'ze war'? Young offers an interesting explanation. The English, he writes, 'laugh to forget'. They resort to humour to blank out the fact that the Second World War, 'despite its constant portrayal as a triumph on British television, at the same time marks the painful nadir. Britain could not have survived the war without sacrificing her Dominions and India [. . .] the loss of her Empire was the price she had to pay for overcoming Germany.' That part of the story is overlooked in British history classes, in spite of their excessive preoccupation with Hitler, Young asserts. 'The loss is drowned out by triumphant cries or laughter.'

Gill would concur. 'That's really the point of English humour,' he writes. 'An awful lot of it is anger in fancy dress.' If that is true then it is easy to see why the tabloids wantonly conflated football and politics before the Turin game in 1990. It came at a time of heightened nervousness in Westminster about German reunification and must have focused English minds on a disquieting suspicion about their neighbours – the sense that they had rather outdone themselves, on and off the pitch, since their last two lost battles, in '45 and '66, while the English had underachieved despite comparable resources.

This failure to keep up with the Schmidts, a failure that *Auf Wiedersehen, Pet* thematised so devastatingly, posed a serious problem for the tabloid agenda. On the one hand it tied in all too well with the narrative of national decline. But at the same time it critically undermined the romanticism of past victories, the mythical golden age that could be juxtaposed with the shambolic present. Just how relevant could '45 and '66 really be when the Germans had so clearly won the peace and almost every other competition since Wembley?

One way out of this dead end was to suggest that nothing had in fact changed. The Germans might have restyled themselves as democratic, peace-loving Europeans but Harry Enfield's 'Jürgen the German' showed that it was all a sham. Jürgen, a tourist in London, profusely apologises 'for my country's behaviour' to anybody who will listen. The merest sign of disorder, however – a bus arriving late, for example – sees him go off on a crazed rant, insisting that 'zis wud never hav happened under ze Germans'. This admittedly hilarious figure was really Winston Churchill's 'Hun' incarnate: 'He is either at your feet or at your throat,' Britain's war hero once memorably declared.

Interestingly enough, the England players seemed unimpressed with the media rabble-rousing and did not afford the Turin game any political significance. In an interview with Christopher Young and Markus Hesselmann of Berlin daily *Der Tagesspiegel*, Gary Lineker admitted in 2006 that the team, all born long after 1945, thought the older generation's obsession with the war was 'understandable but rather amusing'. In the changing room before the match, Lineker had actually put a bet on Bobby Robson mentioning the war in his team talk. 'Robson came in,' Lineker recalled, 'and the first thing he said was, "Lads, think about the war!" Everybody started laughing. Robson asked, "What's going on here?"'

'The Germans have all the qualities the English hold dear: strength, speed, spirit, character and an undying will to win,' noted David Lacey in the *Guardian* on the eve of the 1990 semi-final. It is tempting to speculate that the basic similarity of the two sides' approach (irrespective of the exact tactical set-up), coupled with widely diverging sets of results, have shaped English attitudes towards the Germans over the years just as much as the historical-political context. It is one thing to be beaten by Latins, who for all their deviousness possess 'real', objective skills; another to lose out against a fairly negative side bereft of individual class who essentially do what you are doing, just a little better. Penalties being a perfect case in point. Where is that fabled mettle, that famous resolve, when it is really needed?

Watching the 1994 World Cup in England was a real eye-opener. When the BBC and ITV weren't pretending to love Jack Charlton's Irish Route 1 merchants in the absence of a home nation, they seemed, to this observer at least, unduly concerned with Klinsmann's histrionics and the pedestrian nature of the German team. It was hardly a vintage side, to be sure, but something in the incessant stream of back-handed compliments – we were forever methodical, organised, used to our system, efficient, not beaten until the coach had dropped us off back at the team hotel – seemed a little forced. Subsequent praise for England's dogged defending in the 0–0 World Cup qualifier in Rome in 1997 and the 1–0 victory over Argentina in 2002 – when England scored with a penalty then managed to hold on for dear life by destroying the match altogether in a manner any West German team of the 1980s would have been proud of – exposed the double standard. German organisation: bureaucratic, dull; English organisation: heroic. Ugliness lies in the eye of the beholder. In 2003, a joint poll by the British Council and the German Goethe Institute found that young Brits rated 'bad football' as one of Germany's negative traits, right behind 'role in the Second World War', 'national-socialist past', 'language barrier' and 'bad food' (Young).

The thing with football stereotypes, however, is that there's plenty of fun to be had with them, provided you do not look too closely. Football writer Simon Kuper noted that Germany's 1990 World Cup-winning team, with its many diminutive, predominantly technical players (Thon, Littbarski, Hässler), did not fit the stereotypical view of Germany: eleven automatons who trample over the pitch in straight lines, tackling everybody in their way. One of my Italian colleagues got terribly vexed when an English reporter described Euro 2008's version of the '*Mannschaft*' (team) as typically German. 'What was typical about them?' asked the Italian. 'Their ludicrous frailty at the back? The complete chaos in midfield? Or the skilfully executed one-touch counter-attacking moves?' 'I don't know,' said the Englishman defensively. 'I thought in the end they played the way they always play.'

For reasons that are difficult to ascertain, 'arrogance' seems a watchword, too. It is possible this accusation dates back to Franz Beckenbauer's upright playing style, which was as much a function of his technique – he needed to look down less – as of his position: as the sweeper, the free man, he had a bit more time on the ball to look up. Even in Germany, opposition fans were provoked by the Bayern libero's effortlessness. One threw a knife at him in exasperation. Maybe the origins of the charge can be traced to the 1982 World Cup team. This distinctly unlovable bunch were too busy drinking and playing high-stakes poker to prepare properly for the tournament but arrived in Spain convinced they would leave as world champions. 'We'll score four to eight goals against Algeria to warm up,' announced keeper Harald 'Toni' Schumacher. In fact, his side lost the opener with the North Africans 2–1 and went on to embarrass German football with 'the shame of Gijon', the rigged 1–0 victory over Austria that saw both teams go through. Before they were outclassed by Italy in the final, Schumacher still had time to clatter into Patrick Battiston. The French midfielder lost two teeth and broke his neck, and Schumacher's horror challenge achieved the seemingly impossible: the FC Köln player finished ahead of Adolf Hitler as the most unpopular German in a French poll.

German pre-match confidence may have taken on an air of arrogance in translation, but apart from Andi Möller's ill-advised peacock-strutting at Wembley in 1996 – a reaction to Gascoigne's celebration that the Dortmund player was later ashamed of – it is hard to think of anything specific to support the allegation. Sometimes the facts have simply been wilfully misconstrued. 'Arrogance, typical German arrogance,' tut-tutted Alan Hansen on *Match of the Day* in 2001 when he was told that Germany had already scheduled two friendlies for the dates of the play-offs. The inference was that they considered defeat against England in Munich unfathomable. But the German FA had, of course, merely been pragmatic: calling off friendlies is easily done, arranging them at short notice less so.

The World Cup in Germany seems to have changed a few people's minds, however. For four weeks, Germany – both as a team and a country – showed the world a side of herself she was not convinced she actually had. As Klinsmann's young, fearlessly attacking team pulverised the football stereotypes, millions of their fans were determined to enjoy a peaceful, non-jingoistic, sun-kissed party in black, red and gold. Germany reclaimed patriotism from the radical right that month and found a more natural relationship with itself. Being German became an interesting brand, a kind of lifestyle choice: it became cool. Even in areas with sizeable immigrant communities, the German flag was suddenly everywhere. 'Football achieved what fifty years of politics could not,' wrote *Der Spiegel* about the new spirit of inclusiveness.

The effect this transformation had on the visitors could not have been more remarkable. 'I will support Germany at the next Euros,' proclaimed one football writer after the tournament. The man came from Israel, of all places. One English tabloid hack enjoyed the civility of Baden-Baden, the location of England's team hotel, so much that he came back the following summer with his family. The host's final and best party trick was to let one of the guests leave with the main prize. This new Germany wasn't bad at winning, but it was even better at losing.

The *Independent*'s Sam Wallace could hardly believe his eyes when the entire town of Essen, where he was staying ahead of England's depressingly predictable quarter-final exit in Gelsenkirchen, came to a halt after Germany beat Argentina: 'I was amazed: weren't the Germans just used to winning? Surely this kind of celebration would be more suited to the success-starved English? Many of us assumed that because Germany have won three World Cups, contested a further four finals and generally have a record that us English would weep for, only victory in the summer would suffice. But this was a very different Germany facing the world. Unified and not afraid to show its pride (and maybe a little short of recent successes on the pitch).'

In the stadiums, the old certainties had been kicked into touch as well. 'This World Cup shows no mercy to the clichés,' wrote *Süddeutsche Zeitung* after the last-sixteen round. 'The Germans don't lumber through matches any more, they whoosh from one victory to the next. The Dutch, the old masters of graceful defeats, hack down ideals and opponents, and play out an unspeakable mess. And England? One used to be able to prepare for overwrought expectations and more or less grandiose failure. Now they're winning one sorry match after another. Everything changes at this World Cup, only the English fans stay the same. It's comforting, in a way.'

The English supporters' nostalgic songs were greeted with mild amusement by the German public, for the reasons outlined above. Maybe some people even took pity on them: their past was obviously worth singing about so much more than the present. England were truly woeful. When Ashley Cole threatened that his side were happy 'to play crap all the way to the final' it dawned on many of the foreign reporters in Baden-Baden that England had in fact transformed into 'the Germans' of this tournament. They were slow, one-paced, one-dimensional, over reliant on set pieces. Poor captain Beckham epitomised England's travails: he huffed and puffed but could never close the enormous gap between hype and reality. Physically not in peak condition for the third tournament in a row, Becks was happiest launching diagonal balls from deep inside his own half. This strategy succeeded in nullifying the threat from central midfield and stretched a team that seemed to suffer more than others in the heat. With Beckham unwilling or unable to get to the byline, the right side of England's midfield stopped twenty metres inside the opposition's half.

The English papers were not having a great tournament, either. Their team's uninspiring but on the face of it successful matches amounted to the worst of both worlds. The journalists could not slate the team as long as they were winning nor talk them up as credible contenders as long as they were playing so poorly. Their coverage assumed a muted tone and never built any momentum; it seemed informed by the grim realisation that the end would come sooner or later. England's defeat by Portugal was a bit of a wash-out, too. Inconveniently, there was no obvious villain of the piece on whom the exit in Gelsenkirchen could easily be blamed. Lampard, Gerrard and Carragher all missed their penalties. Rooney was sent off for a silly stamp on Ricardo Carvalho's nether regions. Referee Horacio Elizondo, an Argentinian, had little choice but to show England's talismanic striker the red card. Cristiano Ronaldo had remonstrated with the ref, then winked at his bench afterwards. TV pundit Alan Shearer said he wouldn't be surprised if Rooney smacked Ronaldo after the World Cup. The tabloids did their best to exaggerate the Winker's involvement and a dubious line of defence emerged: apparently, Rooney had been 'too honest'; his frustration stemmed from the fact he hadn't received protection from Elizondo while staying on his feet. It was, by Euro 2004 (Swiss banker ref) and World Cup '98 (Beckham) standards, all very lukewarm stuff. To make matters worse, England could not even be slaughtered for the defeat, as they had played their best game of the tournament with ten men.

The next day, Eriksson raised his hands in front of the press and said he accepted 'the responsibility for everything you want me to' with a wry smile. The blanket confession left everybody even more dejected. Minutes earlier, Beckham had resigned as captain with melodramatic self-pity – 'I have lived the dream' – and just managed to hold back the tears. In the audience, a female Norwegian TV reporter, his most loyal fan at the World Cup, did not succeed in doing so.

Back home, Jeff Powell (*Daily Mail*) and others took what can only be described as the Yoko Ono line: England's players, they complained, had been led astray by the antics of their WAGs (wifes and girlfriends). To be fair, getting a call from your other half at five in the morning – 'Hon, I'm so sloshed' – can't have been conducive to decent performances, but those who despaired about the media circus in Baden-Baden were confusing cause and effect. The WAGs only became the story of the World Cup because England's games themselves had left everybody completely unmoved. (The fact that two dozen news reporters who had been sent to cover any outbreaks of hooliganism found themselves with plenty of time on their hands and nothing else to write about must have played a role, too.)

Nevertheless, Sam Wallace was on to something when he wrote that 'luxurious Baden-Baden, and its legion of WAGs, stood as a symbol of the vapid celebrity that had engulfed Eriksson's England'. A sense of entitlement permeated the camp; 'a culture of complacency' was at work, as Richard Williams noted in the *Guardian*. This air of grandeur was evident in the book deals half the team signed well in advance of the competition, deals that presumed glorious results as a matter of course. It was also, inadvertently, all over the Sky Sports News screens, which on the Sunday morning after the Portugal game informed their viewers that 'England have lost the World Cup'. The curious expression betrayed overconfidence in a team that had entered the tournament as a cross between imagined holders of the title and nailed-on future winners. 'England will get to the final because they deserve it,' Beckham had predicted with more than a touch of hubris. When Michael Owen was injured in the third group game against Sweden, he promised to come back to pick up his winner's medal in Berlin.

'England players have believed for several generations that their reputations alone would be enough to ensure their success,' Williams argued. It was appropriate that the only player who left Baden-Baden with his reputation enhanced was the one who hadn't had one before. Owen Hargreaves, an Englishman born in Calgary, who had undergone his football education in Bavaria, was a joke, as far as the supporters were concerned.

Two months before the World Cup I had been invited to an England fans' forum in London to talk about Germany's expectations for the tournament. One member of the audience brought the house down by asking whether 'that Hargreaves' would make it into the Germany squad. I told them he would. No one believed me.

The papers constantly wondered what Eriksson saw in the Bayern Munich player, who was routinely jeered by his own fans and blanked by his colleagues. The Canuck, as the tabloids called him, did not really fit in, with his slight Canadian accent and lack of Premier League experience. His Bundesliga medals counted for little; the fact that he had won the Champions League as a seventeen-year-old had been long forgotten. The *Sun* called Hargreaves a mass murderer before the tournament. The *Daily Express* thought he might come in handy as a 'tourist guide'.

That view changed when Hargreaves convinced in his natural position as a holding midfielder against Sweden. He even made Gerrard and Lampard look comfortable together. The *Mirror*'s Oliver Holt was moved to offer a '700-word apology'. 'A few weeks ago, I may have given the mistaken impression that I thought Owen Hargreaves was a waste of space,' he wrote. 'That he had no place being in England's World Cup squad. And that he represented the height of Sven Göran Eriksson's folly. Well, I was too hasty making that judgement. Or misjudgement. I hadn't seen him play enough. I was wrong.' Hargreaves excelled again when England were reduced to ten men in Gelsenkirchen. His energy levels were noticeably higher than those of his peers. He showed passion, heart and courage. He alone converted his penalty (with Germanic calmness). A few months later he was voted England's player of the year.

On the England–Germany front, it's been suspiciously quiet since 2006. Two friendlies, at Wembley (2007) and in Berlin (2008), both of which were won 2–1 by the away side, passed off without so much as a whiff of the old 'arrogant Fritz' routine. 'Ze war' seems truly over. For now. Let's see if the peace holds.

Acknowledgements

Thanks to: all the Honigsteins, Feigenbaums and Shavits; Jonathan Wilson, Henry Winter, Rob Draper, Martin Lipton, Sean Ingle, James Gardiner, Kevin McCarra, Gabriele Marcotti, Guillem Balague, Xavier Rivoire, Klaus Hoeltzenbein, Sven Goldmann, Axel Kintzinger, Dr Michael Becker, Martin Mazur, Masumi Tsunoda, Helen Wood, Jim Agnew, David Farrelly, Ben Lyttleton, Marc Fels, Oliver Trust, Oliver Schraft, Philippe Auclair, Mark Scott, James Gardner, Alan McInallay, Metha Punwaratorn, Pirayu Chuenkul, Felix Magath, Moritz Volz, Steffen Freund, Christian Ziege, Didi Hamann, Thomas Hitzlsperger, Robert Huth, Jens Lehmann, Michael Ballack, Matthew Benham, Christoph Biermann, Birgit Schmitz, Tristan Jones.